Fred Dibnah's
Age of Steam

Fred Dibnah's
Age of Steam

Fred Dibnah and David Hall

Acknowledgements
Warm thanks to Natalie Konopinski for research, transcripts and
typing the manuscript and to Clare White for research.

This book is published to accompany the television series
Fred Dibnah's Age of Steam which was first broadcast in 2003.
The series was produced by BBC Factual Entertainment in association
with The View From the North Limited.
Producer: David Hall

First published in 2003.
Copyright © Fred Dibnah and David Hall 2003
The moral right of the authors has been asserted.

ISBN 0 563 48743 7

Published by BBC Worldwide Ltd,
Woodlands, 80 Wood Lane, London W12 0TT

Commissioning editor: Sally Potter
Project editor: Catherine Johnson. Copy editor: Ruth Baldwin
Designer: Linda Blakemore. Picture researcher: Sarah Hopper
Production controller: Kenneth McKay

Set in Meridien by BBC Worldwide Limited
Printed and bound in Great Britain by Butler and Tanner Limited, Frome
Colour separations by Radstock Reproductions Limited, Midsomer Norton
Jacket printed by Lawrence-Allen Limited, Weston-super-Mare

CONTENTS

INTRODUCTION

I developed my great interest in steam a long, long time ago as a small boy living near the railway lines in Bolton when, of course, I used to climb over the fence and do things that little boys shouldn't do. I remember one thing that used to fascinate me; we knew the half-past four 'namer' was coming and we used to put a penny on the line and watch it dance up and down in between all the wheels. When the train had long gone past you went out and collected your penny, which, by this time, was about twice as big as it was before you put it on the railway line. We lived in close proximity to the engine sheds where, on my way home from school, there would be literally dozens of locomotives lined up all steaming and hissing away with water dripping off them and I'd always sneak in and have a look round. Time went by and I ended up actually riding on the things – it was highly illegal, but I had a lot of relations who worked on the railway, which was quite wonderful.

It's strange really, how a person becomes interested in steam. As a little lad I was surrounded by tall chimneys that fascinated me. They all had huge clouds coming out of the top of them – a bit like a Lowry painting – and when you wandered up the back streets you could hear the rumbling inside these great spinning mills. Then later on in my life, when I became a joiner, I used to get really brave and sneak into mill yards and climb up the engine-house steps to look at the engines. I remember as a young lad of about sixteen or seventeen, rather full of fear, looking into the engine-house through the window at the thing going round and seeing the engine minder snoozing in an easy chair. But, you know, he wouldn't really be asleep: he'd be listening for any strange change in the pattern of noise that was coming from the engine, which of course would indicate if something was going wrong.

These big mill engines with massive flywheels were very impressive – imagine a wheel like that, 40 feet (12 m) in diameter and 16 feet (5m) wide with 60 2-inch-diameter (5-cm-diameter) ropes going to wheels up five storeys of spinning mill, all going round almost silently: incredible pieces of machinery! It's sad now when you go to places like Oldham and Rochdale and see all these gaunt, empty engine rooms, very similar to the tin mines in Cornwall. They are just shells, but once they were graced by this beautiful machinery with fancy reeded pillars and handrails and all likes of beautiful brass-work and everything. Lovely! But now they are all gone.

In Bolton we were quite well blessed with steam-engine manufacturers. There were actually three major firms in the town. There was John and Edward Woods, who have a steam engine in Trencherfield Mill at Wigan Pier; then John Musgraves who manufactured all manner of steam engines from pit winding engines to iron-works blowing engines to big textile-mill engines. They, of course, have long faded away, but there are examples of the product still lying about, which are really quite beautiful. In fact, over my cooker in the back kitchen I've got the plate off one of the biggest steam engines that operated in Bolton. The third of these engine manufacturers was Hick, Hargreaves and Company, which was a really old firm started by Benjamin Hick in 1834 or thereabouts. They had a huge works, which was completely demolished to make way for a supermarket. Before the last vestiges of Hick, Hargreaves had hit the deck, the roof was being put on the supermarket.

It's sad now when you look around Bolton. Even in my short lifetime – and none of us is around for very long – many changes have come about. The interesting machinery that used to be around has all but disappeared completely. When I was a lad, there were 200 factory chimneys sticking up in between rows of houses. It was an incredible skyline, and of course most other industrial towns in Lancashire and the northern half of England were pretty much the same. What you've got to think is that at the bottom of every one of those chimneys was a steam engine of one sort or another. A steam engine is virtually indestructible, some of them were literally made in James Watt's period back in the eighteenth century. There's a great mill in Bolton called the Gilner Mill that was still driven right up to 1947 by a beam engine with Watt's parallel motion.

A steam engine really is a fascinating thing. When it is running it comes alive in a strange way. It has an unbelievable smell about it for a start. Even people who come to my garden now notice it when they go near my boiler. We had an old guy come in the other day, eighty-odd years old, and he was sniffing away and he said, 'That brings back memories of my youth.' Oil and steam have a smell all of their own. It has been said that if you could put it in a bottle and cork it up you could sell it – it smells that good.

Then there's the noise that the engines made. Some of them were very quiet, but it depended on what sort they were and where they were and what sort of job they were doing. If you've got a colliery winding engine, winding in a shaft that was 800 yards (732 m) deep, with a cage hanging on the end of a rope with maybe 10 tons of coal in it and the engine's got to start from a standstill, it would make a heck of a racket. In the middle of a place called Leigh near Bolton, there was a pit known as Parsonage. There was a winding engine there that you could hear in the next town down the road when it set off. And what a sight it was. The roar of it into the clouds and a great cloud of steam over the top of the engine house! I think modern man has missed something in not seeing that sort of vision.

The boiler in my back garden makes the steam for turning a little steam engine round, and that engine drives all the machinery that I've got there. It all comes in handy, particularly for rebuilding the traction engine I'm working on. I've been restoring this engine for nearly twenty years and, despite some major setbacks, it's now nearly ready for the road. Just a bit more time and I'll be able to complete the job. It's going to be an unbelievable sense of achievement getting it finished, because by then I will have built the whole thing myself from scratch, with a complete new boiler and it will all have been done with the power of steam.

People say I'm eccentric running all the old machinery I have in my back garden, but it's more modern than some of the things I've come across that people have working for them in their back gardens.

I know one man in Staffordshire who's built a windmill in his – that's really going back to an old-fashioned way of generating power. You've got to be pretty confident in your own abilities to take on something like that, but it's nothing to the confidence of the great pioneering engineers of the eighteenth and nineteenth centuries who built the first railways and the first iron steamships.

It took confidence on a massive scale, in the days of wooden-hulled ships, to build an ocean liner of metal, which was powered by steam. But Isambard Kingdom Brunel had a faith in himself and his abilities that was amazing even by the standards of his day. The Victorian age was one in which Britain led the world in the skills of making and inventing things. It was a time when the skills of mechanics and engineers were highly prized: the Age of Steam, when British industry led the world. Engineers were the heroes of the day whose exploits captured the imagination of the Victorian public. They were treated like pop stars or footballers are now. For me the greatest of the lot, my hero, was Brunel. He dominated every field of engineering – railway-building, civil engineering, ship-building, bridge-building – and nothing seemed to be beyond his capacity. For a man like Brunel, no challenge was too great: throwing dramatic bridges across great rivers and gorges; building an iron steamship that would have to carry tons of coal across the Atlantic without sinking; digging a tunnel under the River Thames.

All this was made possible in the second half of the eighteenth century when there was a series of technological breakthroughs in the field of iron-working and in experiments in the use of steam power. These resulted in the invention of machinery that revolutionized the various processes in the manufacture of textiles. Yet, in spite of these technological breakthroughs, before Queen Victoria came to the throne Britain was still an agricultural land. It was still by and large the old world of stagecoaches, pack horses, highwaymen, sailing ships, water power and human effort. But the application of the new technology to transport, with the development of the world's first successful railways just before her reign began, meant that between her coronation and her death Victoria saw Britain change beyond recognition.

As well as seeing the country linked by railways, she witnessed sail give way to steam at sea and industry spread its smoky cities all over Britain. What made it all happen was the vast quantities of coal and iron ore that became available during the course of Victoria's reign, enabling the new technology to be harnessed and turning Britain from a land of farmers to an industrial giant dominating the world and ruling over a vast empire. The rise of manufacturing, mining, trade and transport brought a big increase in national prosperity and transformed the appearance of the country. The pithead winding gear of coal mines began to appear all over the land to provide the fuel for this great industrial expansion.

It was the age of the engineer; an age when men of great vision, energy and self-belief could flourish. These architects of change became the most important figures of the Victorian age. And it was the building of the railways that gave them their greatest opportunities. With the opening of the line linking Liverpool and Manchester in 1830, the railway era had begun in earnest. By the time Victoria came to the throne in 1837, armies of navvies were being employed building the railways. Railways became the great symbol of Victorian industrial and technical ingenuity, which formed the basis of the prosperity of the country at this time. It was an exciting period when anything seemed to be possible. It was the Age of Steam.

Of course, the development of the steam engine carried on right up to the 1920s when it became obvious that the steam turbine was a much better piece of equipment and much more economical. In fact, the steam turbine is still our main source of electricity. Its invention revolutionized electricity generation and, although he's nothing like as well known, the man who invented it, Charles Parsons, and his steam turbine were to the twentieth century what James Watt and the steam engine were to the nineteenth.

Steam locomotives continued to be built and operated on the railways until the 1960s and many of the great steam-driven mill engines and colliery winding engines were used until the same time to provide direct steam power. But as transport and industry turned more and more to electrical power it was still steam that was at the heart of the power-generating process. And so it continues right up to today. Even the modern nuclear power station relies on steam. In a nuclear power station the turbine blades that are used to generate the electricity are driven by steam in very much the same way as those in a coal-fired power station. The main difference is that a nuclear plant uses uranium contained in metal fuel rods instead of coal as a fuel to make the steam. The fuel rods in a nuclear power station fill exactly the same function as the coal in my traction engine – basically they both heat the water, which raises the steam, which provides the power to drive the engines.

So the Age of Steam isn't dead yet. In fact, engineers and scientists are looking at steam power again because, with growing concern over the build-up of toxic and smog-producing gases created by the internal combustion engine, people are looking for more environmentally friendly technologies for transport. And one of the answers could be steam. A new generation of British engineers and scientists has become interested in steam and is now building a steam-powered car to mount a challenge on the world land speed record for a steam-powered vehicle. As well as breaking the record, the aim is also to create interest in the use of alternative fuels.

At the height of the Industrial Revolution and for much of the twentieth century the fuel used for the steam engine was coal, and it was the coal that caused all the pollution, not the steam engine itself. A steam engine isn't reliant on coal. In fact it's not fuel-specific, which means that any fuel can be used for it, including the cleanest that is available: direct sunlight. The vehicle being developed for the world land-speed record incorporates leading-edge technologies to create a fast, efficient environmentally friendly method of transport. The project couples the wealth of steam technology gained from the eighteenth century onwards with some of the most advanced technologies known to man today. And it's not all as far-fetched as it might seem. As long ago as 1906, a steam-powered car was driven at the amazing speed of 127 miles per hour (204 kmph). So, with today's technologies the target of 200 miles per hour (321 kmph) for the new record is attainable. With developments like this going on, perhaps the twenty-first century will be the new Age of Steam.

CHAPTER ONE

THE EARLY PIONEERS

Steam power was the driving force behind the Industrial Revolution. It developed out of an ever-increasing need to pump water from mines to enable miners to dig deeper. At first this was performed by human beings and animals – reasonably efficient for a time but, by the end of the seventeenth century, as populations grew and towns expanded, there was an increasing need to get more and more raw materials like coal, tin and iron ore. There had to be another source of power for the pumping operations. Steam was the answer.

The steam engine is really a fairly simple machine. The principles of steam power are based around two major properties. First, the expansion of steam in an enclosed cylinder pushing a piston which is connected to a crankshaft by a connecting rod. And second, the sudden condensation of steam, which creates a vacuum in the cylinder, making it easier for the steam to push the piston back along the cylinder to its starting place.

Thomas Newcomen invented the first successful steam engine in 1705, but later in the eighteenth century it was greatly improved by James Watt. Before this time, though, it had been known for many centuries that steam was capable of moving a mass. From the ancient world up to the beginning of the Industrial Revolution men of science had tried to find ways of harnessing it in some way.

The first steam engine for which we have any record was devised by a Greek mathematician, Hero of Alexandria. No one is sure of the exact date when he lived, but historians have deduced from his writings that it was during the first century AD. Hero wrote a number of books about ingenious inventions, gadgets and magical tricks. One of these included his description of the very first idea for a steam engine, including multiple pulleys, cogwheels and levers.

His interests were in mechanics and engineering and he came up with a wonderful piece of tackle like a sphere with two exhaust pipes, one on top and one underneath. This sphere was supported by two brackets standing on the lid of a basin of boiling water. When the steam was produced, it squirted out of the two exhaust pipes and caused the thing to revolve. The movement of the ball was used to make puppets dance: you could call it the very first mechanical toy that actually revolved. It must have been a weird thing – a bit like a sputnik; a kind of very early jet engine. It was only in the light of what followed eighteen centuries later that Hero's *aeolipyle*, as it was called, was recognized as a simple form of steam turbine.

Hero also described and sketched a method of opening temple doors by means of steam power, which is quite a wonderful thing. This ingenious device, which he wrote about in his book *Spiritalia*, contained many of the elements of the modern steam engine. And this

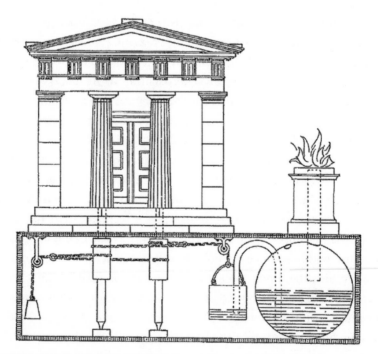

Above: Hero's design for opening the temple doors.

was nearly 2,000 years ago! Basically, the way it worked was that beneath the temple doors was a spherical vessel containing water. A pipe connected the upper part of the sphere with the hollow shell of the altar above, which was airtight. To open the doors you lit a fire on the altar, which heated the air inside a box. The heated air would expand and this, in turn, would force water up a pipe and into a bucket. When the bucket was full of water, it descended, turning a number of barrels as it did, which in turn would raise a counterbalance on the end of a rope and this would open the doors. When the fire was extinguished, the air condensed inside the chamber and forced the water by vacuum up a pipe and back into the sphere. This caused the counterbalance weight to shut the doors again. It was a very clever piece of tackle. Whether Hero ever made one nobody knows, but the drawings he produced for it still exist.

In the ancient world experiments like this were carried out more as a sort of novelty to achieve 'surprising results'. There was no need or wish to use the power of steam for any real practical purpose or material benefit. It was for magic and religion, not industry and the economy, that experiments were carried out. Ingenuity was much more prized than any material gain or practicality. So, in spite of these amazing spectacles, it was another 1,500 years before anybody tried to make any serious investigations into the application of steam power.

The next record we have of the practical use of steam is from 1543 when a Spanish naval officer, Blasco de Garay, turned his attention to propelling ships by steam. He reputedly sailed a boat called the *Trinity* across the harbour of Barcelona by steam power. However, like a lot of old inventors, he was very guarded about his work and he did things with a great deal of secrecy, so nobody really knows whether what is written down actually happened or not. He refused to let anyone know how his ship worked, but apparently it contained a large copper boiler and paddle-wheels, which were suspended over the sides of the vessel. When the *Trinity* sailed in a trial, some people approved but others said it was too slow. Of course, boiler technology then was quite poor and it could have been very dangerous. Yet however primitive it was and however many drawbacks it had, it was the first recorded attempt to put steam to a practical use in propelling a vessel.

Another important development in the sixteenth century was recorded by an Italian called Giambattista della Porta. Born in 1535, he had been well educated at home by private tutors and is described as a mathematician, chemist, physicist and engineer; a gentleman of fortune and an enthusiastic student of science, a 'natural philosopher'. Della Porta was able to devote most of his time to study because he'd never had any real need to work on account of his family's wealth. He lived in Naples and his home became a meeting place for all sorts of students, artists and men who were distinguished in every branch of science. In his nineteenth book of 'natural magick' he described a machine that made water rise. It was a very similar idea to Hero's temple-door-opening machine and he may have copied it from him, but instead of using hot air, della Porta employed steam pressure to force liquid out of a closed container. He called his new machine an improved 'Hero's fountain' and he named it his 'steam fountain'. He was the first person to describe the action of condensation creating a vacuum, and he made sketches for a device in which the vacuum was filled by water,

Below left: This is della Porta's piece of apparatus which demonstrated the expansive power of steam.
Below right: de Caus's sphere.

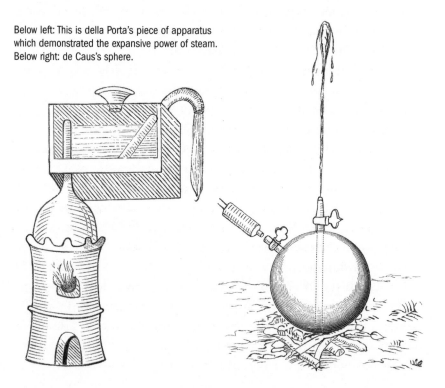

which was forced in by the external atmospheric pressure. Apparently this was never put to any useful mechanical purpose.

Around the same time in 1605, a French landscape gardener called Solomon de Caus, whose work took him to England, Italy and Germany, invented a machine that would, in his own words 'demonstrate that water will mount by help of fire higher than its own level'. It was a sphere like Hero's, but instead of turning round and round it just squirted water up into the sky, which would have been quite a novelty for the rich people who employed him to make fountains, pumps and waterwheels for their gardens.

Like the other inventors before him, de Caus never really discovered any practical use for his steam fountain. But he was one of the first men to be involved in the pumping of water and it was this that proved to be the turning point in the development of steam power, because pumping water was one of the great challenges of the eighteenth century. This was the period when removing water from deep mines became important for the wealth of the nation.

All over Europe the growing economic importance of mining had been turning the search for a way to harness the power of steam into a necessity. In Italy in 1641 Cosimo de Medici, Grand Duke of Tuscany, required his engineers to make a suction pump that would draw water from a depth of 50 feet (15 m). When they found that the water wouldn't rise further than about 25 feet (7.5 m) up their pipe, leaving an unfilled vacuum above, they asked the great inventor, Galileo, for an explanation. His reply was that it needed a lot more investigation, which others should do. The philosophers and scientists who carried out the investigation thought, at first, that wherever there was a vacuum, air or water would rush to fill it. But when they found that water didn't rush to fill the vacuum in the pipe, they realized that air has weight and can exert pressure. Water rose in a pipe because it was pushed, but would only go as high as the level where it balanced with air. The demonstration of 'the spring and weight of the air' was made in Italy by Evangelista Torricelli and Vincenzio Viviani, both followers of Galileo. It was also made in France by Blaise Pascal in 1647, and in Germany by a scientist called Otto von Guericke, who was mayor of Madgeburg.

A particularly dramatic demonstration to show that the atmosphere was a source of power was carried out by von Guericke in 1654, using a piston-and-cylinder apparatus. In this the cylinder stood upright with the open end to the top and a rod from a piston protruding. A strong rope attached to the piston rod was taken over a pulley above and twenty men pulled the piston up the cylinder to hold it against the partial vacuum they created. Guericke connected the base to a copper sphere, from which all the air had been pumped out. Then the cocks on the connecting pipe were opened and the residual air in the cylinder rushed into the space with so much power that the piston was driven down and the twenty men were all pulled over.

It was clear from this that a powerful engine that was independent of human, animal, water or wind power could be built, but needed to obtain a vacuum under the piston in some way besides an air pump – which is what von Guericke had used. The search for alternatives included trying gunpowder, but about a fifth of the air was still left in the cylinder, so it didn't really work. In the meantime, steam provided an answer and it came from an English lord.

All of this, so far, had been mere experimentation. Nobody had yet built anything resembling a steam engine that had done any useful work. Edward Somerset, the second Marquis of Worcester, is reputed to be the first man to build a steam engine and demonstrate the expansive properties of steam in a more practical way. Worcester is described as being a learned, thoughtful, studious and good man; a Romanist (that is, a Roman Catholic) without prejudice or bigotry; a loyal subject and honourable public figure. He was a mechanic of wonderful ingenuity and of clear, almost intuitive apprehension.

In 1663 he produced a curious collection of descriptions of his inventions, as he called it, and one of these involved raising water by steam. The way it worked was that steam was generated in a boiler that went through a pipe into a vessel filled with water. When the steam came in, it forced the water out of a pipe. The vessel was then shut off from the boiler and the whole process was repeated by filling up the vessel with water again. This method was actually used for raising water at Vauxhall in London, but the Marquis did not make any money out of it. He never managed to succeed in setting up the company that he would have needed to operate on a proper commercial basis and, in spite of the fact that he started out as a wealthy and influential man, he spent a fortune on his experiments until he was left penniless, with no home. His fate was that of nearly all inventors of the time: he ended up poor and unsuccessful.

From the time of the Marquis of Worcester onwards, steam development entered a new stage, which was one of application rather than mere experimentation. During the reign of Charles II there was a great growth of activity in the field of applied science. The King himself had a laboratory built and he employed learned men to carry out experiments. It was the first stage of Britain attaining a superiority over the continent that was to blossom with the Industrial Revolution. Around this time, towards the end of the seventeenth century, English miners were digging deeper and deeper and the problem of how to clear water from their shafts was becoming almost insurmountable. Something had to be done about it. The experiments of a French doctor called Dionysius Papin and the practical application of known principles by an Englishman, Thomas Savery, gave them the machinery that they needed.

Papin was a key figure in the story of steam. Although he came from a Protestant family, he was educated in the school of the Jesuits at Blois, which is where he acquired his knowledge of maths. He went on to study medicine in Paris and settled there in 1672 with the intention of practising his profession. Apparently he devoted all his spare time to studying physics and moved to London in 1678 to pursue his studies. Papin became one of the most celebrated engineers of his day and took his place among the most talented and famous of mechanics. He invented the pressure cooker, christening it the 'digester'. This really put him at the forefront of controlling pressurized steam. Food would be cooked in water that was heated by a fire, and the pressure was determined and limited by a weight on the safety valve lever.

In 1687 Papin produced the first piston steam engine. For a long time scientists had been looking at ways to create a vacuum into which a piston could move. Papin was the first man to use an air pump to pump the air out. This enabled the atmospheric pressure to push the piston back the other way into the vacuum in the cylinder and lift a weight. But he wanted to create a better vacuum, so he used steam to displace the air and used condensation to create the vacuum. When he did this, he really produced the first mechanical steam engine and the first piston steam engine in which condensation was produced to create a vacuum. His experiment involved a small brass cylinder 2½ inches (6 cm) in diameter, fitted with a piston. Water was boiled in the bottom of this cylinder and the resulting steam went to the top where it was held by a catch. When the fire was removed the steam condensed, causing a partial vacuum, and, once the catch was released, the piston went down with sufficient force to raise a weight of 60 lbs (27 kg) by a cord and pulley. With these experiments successfully completed, Papin put his inventive mind to a new engine to drive a waterwheel and later on to another form of power to drive ships. But none of these was a success and he died in about 1712, an unhappy and disheartened man, without seeing any of his wonderful ingenious inventions put to any form of use.

Thomas Savery was next on the scene and he was the first man to invent and design an engine that was actually used for pumping water out of mines. From a well-known Devonshire family, he was born at Shilston around 1650. Well educated, he became a military engineer. He was very fond of mathematics, mechanics and natural philosophy and he spent a lot of his time experimenting, inventing and creating things. One of his first inventions, which he patented, was a device for propelling ships in calm weather. This amounted to two paddlewheels and a capstan: when the wind wasn't bending the sails, the lads on deck could turn the capstan and the paddles went round. He offered this to the Admiralty but they decided that it was too slow and were not interested in it.

From this moment on, Savery concentrated on developing steam pumping gear. He'd noted the constant and expensive engineering problems that were involved in keeping mine shafts free of water, and in 1698 he invented what he called his 'fire engine'. This was a steam pump for draining water from mine shafts. It consisted of a furnace heating a boiler, which was connected by pipes to two copper receivers. From the bottom of these receivers branch pipes turned upwards and were united to form a raising main or 'forcing pipe'. Then from the top of each receiver there was also a pipe, which was turned downwards, and these pipes united to form a suction pipe, which was led to the bottom of the shaft from where the water was to be drawn. The maximum lift was 24 feet (7.3 m).

In 1702 he began marketing the engine as the *Miner's Friend*, but of course the deeper the mine shaft, the more dangerous the business of playing around with steam became, and the mine owners were quite worried about it. The problems arose when water needed to be raised from any considerable depth, because the pressure of steam required would cause the engine to blow up, and they only had poor-quality materials to make boilers out of – it was a recipe for disaster and there were quite a few fatalities. Savery spent a lot of time experimenting with boilers and the like to try to perfect the engine, but he never fitted his boilers with safety valves. This was something that only came later.

One of the big advantages of Savery's engine was that it was capable of a continuous delivery because the boiler could be refilled without stopping the engine. A second, smaller boiler was heated to provide a higher pressure of steam than that in the engine itself, and the water forced by steam pressure into the main boiler. But these engines consumed a lot of fuel. They were not economical because the boilers were of such simple form and the heating surface was too small.

Below: Thomas Savery's engine. Savery was the first to design an engine that was capable of pumping water out of mines.

Savery was the very first inventor to try to market a steam engine and, unlike a lot of other inventors at that time, he was very open about his work and liked everybody to know how his machines worked. He also found other uses for his steam engine, such as pumping water for towns, large estates and country houses. In another, more simple engine that he built at Kensington, he followed the same general plan but combined it with a suction pipe. The engine included a single receiver capable of containing 13 gallons (60 litres) of water, a boiler with a 40-gallon (182-litre) capacity and a forcing pipe with connecting pipe and cogs. The Kensington engine cost £50 and raised 3,000 gallons (13,638 litres) per hour, filling the receiver four times a minute. But the Kensington engine was too small for the coal mines. It could have been used for domestic purposes like watering the garden but Savery did not sell this type of engine. It was the later and more efficient engine the *Miner's Friend* that became a real commercial concern.

All sorts of rumours were put out about Savery: that he was heavily influenced by Papin and that he had seen the Marquis of Worcester's engine and basically copied his idea. It is also said that he bought up all the books he could find on the subject of steam power and burned them so that nobody would find out where he got his information. Another story claims that Savery had discovered the enormous power of steam by chance and, to cover it up, he invented a tale about how he filled a wine glass with steam and plunged it upside down into a vessel full of water. Of course, when the steam condensed, the atmospheric pressure caused the wine glass to fill with water. If you just got a wine glass and shoved it upside down into a tub of water, the air would be contained inside and no water would go inside it, as with a diving bell.

Whether or not these stories are true, in 1699 Savery certainly demonstrated a model of his steam pump to the Royal Society. It was the first time that a steam-powered engine had been shown to a learned society and it was met with approval. The machine had no moving parts except for hand-operated steam and water cocks and it was basically a steam pump operating on the principle described by Della Porta. But the distinct advantage over previous engines was that it also used atmospheric pressure to drive water up a suction pipe and into a receiver ready to be forced out again and up the delivery pipe when steam was next admitted from the boiler.

Savery faced the same problem as the engineers of Cosimo de Medici: that you couldn't raise water by atmospheric pressure for more than about 25 feet (7.5 m). To resolve this a different pump would be needed every 25 or 30 feet (7.5 or 9 m) down the shaft. This would have been expensive and dangerous – all these boilers part-way down under the ground. Another problem was the energy loss, which came about from steam being brought into direct contact with cold water in the receiver. Savery's most obvious failure was with an engine he installed at York Buildings near the Strand in London to replace a waterwheel under London Bridge. The waterwheel was used to pump Thames water to supply homes and buildings for people in Picadilly and Whitehall. Savery's engine was installed in 1712 for the same purpose. But the engine used steam at pressures higher than the pipework could stand, so it had to be taken out of use. But Savery still remained a pioneer in the eyes of his contemporaries.

At the end of the eighteenth century Savery's engines were still being used in Leeds in a flax mill and in a number of cotton mills. The interesting thing here is that the actual steam engine wasn't used to drive the machinery but to raise the water, and it was the waterwheel that did the driving of the machinery. In other words, they recycled the water: possibly during the night they would pump it up into a reservoir and then use the wheel during the day. The principle is very similar to that of modern hydroelectric stations where they generate all day and pump the water back up all night when the demand for power is not there. As late as 1820 a Savery engine was employed to work a waterwheel turning machinery in an engineering works in Kentish Town in London.

But in spite of all these developments, until 1712 the 'engines' that were available for pumping water from flooded mines were totally inadequate. The owners of coal and tin mines just couldn't keep up with the problems caused by water, which cut into profits, threatened jobs and claimed human lives without warning, especially where shafts were sunk along the coastline and extended under the sea. This was particularly the case in Cornwall. One traveller to the county in the late eighteenth century wrote: 'They even work on the Lord's Day to keep the mines open – one thousand men and boys working on the drainage of twenty mines.' Even so, the sea frequently won, as dozens of mines were lost to the waves.

The problems of water pumping and drainage had been met with varying degrees of success throughout history since the early empires of Babylon and Egypt. The early 'chain of pots' system of drainage used then hadn't changed much by the eighteenth century. Power to drive this sort of bucket elevator system could be provided by man, beast, wind or water, each of which was either inefficient or unreliable. Certainly this method couldn't cope with the pressing drainage problems that faced the coal owners and the Cornish tin-mine owners at the start of the eighteenth century. The search for a more efficient and reliable source of power for draining mines was the most pressing technological problem of the time. And so the steam engine was born.

By the beginning of the eighteenth century all the known elements of the modern steam engine had been discovered. They'd each been put to individual use and all that remained was for some really good inventor to screw everything together into a practical machine capable of using the power of steam economically. Thomas Newcomen, who came to be known as the 'father of the steam engine', provided the great step forward that was needed. Born into an aristocratic family that had fallen on hard times, he ran an ironmonger's shop in Dartmouth, Devon. In the 1680s he formed a partnership with a man called John Calley. Calley was a local plumber and he and Newcomen toured the tin mines of Devon and Cornwall providing the mine owners with iron and doing plumbing and blacksmithing jobs for them on site. On these tours they were able to see the problem of flooding for themselves at first hand.

In 1710, with Calley's assistance, Newcomen designed an engine for pumping water at Helston in Cornwall. This first attempt was a failure – it didn't work properly – but during the next two years he invented an entirely new kind of engine, which he called the 'atmospheric engine'. What we all breathe every day is the atmosphere, or air, which has a pressure of about 15 lbs per square inch (1 kg per cm^2). The atmospheric engine uses this power to its advantage. An atmospheric engine is basically an open-ended cylinder with a piston in it and a piston rod protruding out of the top. Steam is introduced into the cylinder and then cold water condenses the steam, creating a vacuum below the piston. Then the atmosphere, at 15 lbs per square inch (1 kg per cm^2), pushes the piston down to the bottom, lifting up the beam and sending the pump rods down the shaft. Then it goes back by gravity the other way and the same thing happens again: the steam goes into the cylinder, the water condenses it, the vacuum is caused and it pushes the piston down one more time. Newcomen's engine did eight to ten strokes a minute and its own valve gear controlled it automatically. Unlike Savery, Newcomen didn't make use of the expansive properties of steam. Instead he used it to create the vacuum and then let atmospheric pressure do the work, hence the name 'atmospheric engine'. The advantage was that he didn't have to control high-pressure steam. The Newcomen engine was designed for one purpose alone – to pump water from mine shafts and mines. The first example was installed at a colliery in Staffordshire and it was an unbelievable success. It proved to be the world's first successful steam engine, and over the next fifty years Newcomen engines were installed all over England and the Continent.

Little is known about Newcomen himself other than that he was a fairly humble man who wasn't held in very high esteem, even among his own people. He was classed as an eccentric sort of inventor. Newcomen certainly owed a lot to the men who came before him. Papin can be credited as the first to develop the idea of the use of steam and Savery actually invented and patented an engine that had been used for pumping water from mines. Newcomen took the idea of Papin's cylinder and piston and married it up with Savery's principle of condensing steam. The end product, the actual engine that he built, was so much like Savery's that Savery was only stopped from taking him to court because Newcomen made him a partner.

Basically, Newcomen's engine evolved from the principle of the common hand pump that was used to bring water up from a well. With a hand pump the hand is applied to a rod connected with a pivoted lever. As the rod is pushed down by the hand, the plunger, which is fixed to the other end of the lever, is raised so that it discharges water from the spout of the pump. What Newcomen did was to replace the human hand with a simple steam-powered piston and cylinder. The device he invented was an ingenious combination of what would soon become familiar elements of the industrial age: a piston and cylinder, pumps, valves, levers and a process of producing low pressure by the condensation of steam in a vessel.

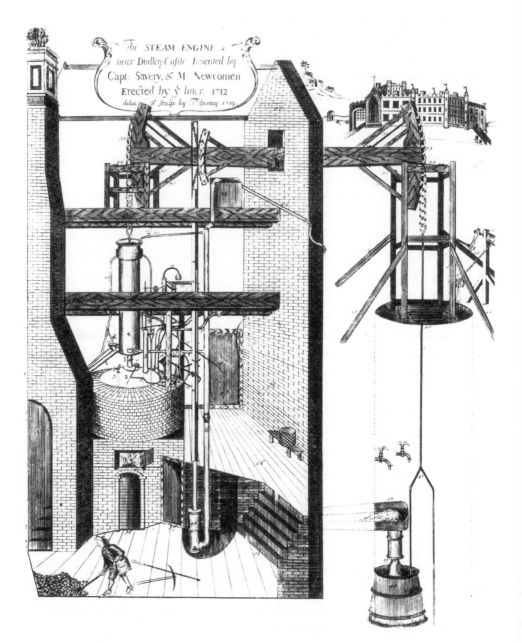

The STEAM ENGINE
near Dudley Castle Invented by
Capt: Savery, & Mr. Newcomen
Erected by ye later. 1712
delin: & sculp by T. Barney 1719.

Above: Newcomen's engine installed at Dudley Castle, Wolverhampton in 1712.

Newcomen produced his first successful working model in 1705, but by 1712 he'd made the real thing and installed it at Dudley Castle in Tipton near Wolverhampton. It marked the beginning of the Steam Age proper. Rather than lift water itself, his engine was applied to work conventional pumps. It was more intricate than Savery's but made less extreme demands and so was the first successful engine.

Within a few years of its invention Newcomen's engine had been introduced into nearly all the existing big mines in Britain and was an enormous success. Many new mines, which couldn't have been worked at all previously, were opened when it was found that this engine could be relied upon to raise the large quantities of water that needed to be removed. It enabled miners to sink to twice the depth they had been able to previously. Within ten years of its invention the atmospheric engine was in operation all over Europe.

But Newcomen's engine had a number of weaknesses. First of all, the fire was several feet deep, which meant that combustion was inefficient. Then, because the cylinder had to be heated and cooled for each stroke, the engine was not very efficient and consumed large quantities of fuel. There was also the problem of the pressure the boiler could stand: the technology of the boiler construction required gaps to be packed with iron filings, which meant that boiler explosions were common. As well as this, the strokes of the machine were very slow because the steam was condensed by applying water to the outside of the container.

Then one day the engineers noticed the strokes moving very quickly. Newcomen was called in and after a search he found a hole in the piston, which let cold water in. He had accidentally discovered that a small jet of cold water introduced into the single piston as it reaches a full head of steam causes the resulting air pressure to push the piston down, which in turn raises the suction pump rod, lifting the ground water to the surface. Within weeks he had redesigned his engine so that this accident occurred precisely once every stroke.

The Newcomen engine was constructed directly above the mine shaft, with its giant metal cylinder encased in a circular brick boiler house that towered over the men who kept it stoked up. It was a very inefficient piece of equipment really, but it worked which was the main thing. Some of the largest engines that were built gobbled up over 30 tons of fuel, in the form of coal, at one go. But this didn't matter very much – certainly in the case of coal mines, because that was a substance they had plenty of. Even right up to modern times boiler plants at many collieries were very inefficient.

And, old as they are, it is still possible to see a working Newcomen engine today. When the Newcomen Society for the Study of the History of Engineering and Technology decided to create a suitable memorial to Thomas Newcomen on the occasion of the tercentenary of his birth, the British Transport Commission donated a small engine to them very similar to the 1712 Dudley Castle engine. The engine had been standing idle for around fifty years, but it was dismantled, removed from its site and re-erected at Dartmouth in Devon where it is on show in a newly constructed engine house. Dating from 1725, it is a direct descendant of Newcomen's first machine and displays many of the features of the early version. You can see a similar engine at Elsecar, near Barnsley in South Yorkshire. It's a Newcomen-type pumping engine, believed to date from between 1787 and 1795, and, although it's no longer working, it is claimed to be one of Britain's finest surviving legacies of the Industrial Revolution. The engine operated continuously as an efficient system of mines drainage until 1923. Ironically, it was briefly brought out of retirement in 1928 when the electrically operated pumps that were introduced to replace it were put out of action by floodwater! Although damaged in 1953 and no longer having a source of steam, it is still technically workable and now holds pride of place at Elsecar.

In the Black Country there's a wonderful reproduction of a Newcomen engine, which actually works. It's really good. We've had it going once or twice. It's very slow and is actually quite a frightening thing when you see it working, with a lot of levers and things that are similar to the rotating mechanisms in clocks. You can imagine when Cornwall was full of engines of this nature.

At a colliery between Ashton-under-Lyne and Oldham, not far from where I live in Lancashire, I hear tell that there were the remains of an original atmospheric engine called *Fairbottom Bobs*. The engine was used to drain water from the Cannel coal pits, which were about 200 feet

(61 m) deep, close to the River Medlock, about half a mile from Park Bridge, Ashton-under-Lyne. It got its name from the bobbing motion of the wooden beam. The water was pumped along a wooden trough to top up the level of the Fairbottom Branch canal, 200 yards (183 m) away at Fenny Fields Bridge. The engine was in use until 1834. Photographs were taken of it in the 1880s and it was often mistaken for 'Watt's first engine'.

In 1929 Henry Ford visited Trafford Park in Manchester to have a look at his newly created Ford motor works. While he was there he heard about this engine at Ashton-under-Lyne and he went to look at it. He decided to buy it there and then, and took it back to America where he installed it in a museum that he owned. On the same visit he saw a steam wagon going down the street in Manchester and he flagged the guy down and bought that as well and took that back to America where it was displayed for many years in the Henry Ford Motor Museum. Recently, though, a collector in the north of England heard the museum was selling it and he's now brought it back to this country.

At a place near my home just outside Bolton, there's a wonderful creation that's obviously home made, using the beam off an old engine. I wouldn't say it was an atmospheric one, but it's very old, and it's actually driven by a waterwheel with a crank and a connecting rod to one end of the beam. At the other end of the beam there's a piston rod into a cylinder which pumps water from the River Irwell up to a lagoon at a paper mill at Radcliffe – or at least it used to. It's derelict now, though the remains are all there, slightly overgrown but still recognizable.

That sort of thing gives a good idea of the many and varied uses that the Newcomen engine was put to. Its main one, of course, was pumping water from mines, but it was also used for supplying towns with water, pumping it for the local populace and big houses and the like. It was even tried for the propulsion of ships, but it wasn't very successful and was even quite dangerous, so it was abandoned for that use for quite a long time afterwards.

In the search for greater power, engineers before James Watt had tended to concentrate on increasing the size of the cylinder or installing two or more boilers per cylinder to achieve a more regular supply of steam. In 1774 John Smeaton, the most distinguished engineer of the time, began to build engines with steam cylinders of greater length of stroke than had been customary. He gave a greater excess of pressure on the steam side, which enabled him to increase the speed of the piston considerably. The first of his new style of engines was built at Long Benton, near Newcastle upon Tyne, in 1774. In total fifty-seven of his engines were eventually built there. Smeaton covered the lower side of his steam pistons with a wooden plank 2¼ inches (5.7 cm) thick to absorb the heat where the iron was directly exposed to the steam. This meant that less of the heat was wasted.

As well as building his own engines, Smeaton also made the first duty trials of existing engines. He made a number of test trials of Newcomen engines to determine the expenditure of fuel required to raise a defined quantity of water to a stated height. He found that an engine with a cylinder that had a 10-inch-diameter (25-cm-diameter) and a stroke of 3 feet (90 cm) could do work equal to raising 2,919,017 lbs (1,324,066 kg) of water 1 foot (30 cm) high with a bushel of coals weighing 82 lbs (37 kg). By means of these tests he was able to determine proper proportions and, as a result, he introduced many changes, some of which doubled engine performance.

Smeaton built one of his engines at the Chasewater mine in Cornwall in 1775 with a maximum piston stroke of 9 feet (2.7 m). The pumps were in three lifts of about 100 feet (30.5 m) each, with nine strokes being made per minute. In 1780 Smeaton had eighteen large engines working in Cornwall. By the end of the eighteenth century the engine that had been developed initially by Newcomen had been perfected by Smeaton's systematic study and research and had become a well-established form of steam engine. Smeaton is something of a forgotten figure in the history of the steam engine, but he made many important advances. As early as 1765 he designed a small, portable engine on a wooden frame mounted on short legs. This was assembled so the whole machine could be transported and set to work wherever it was needed. In place of a beam, a large pulley was used, over which a chain was carried. This connected the piston with the pump rod. The boiler was shaped like a large tea kettle.

By the late eighteenth century the steam engine had been introduced and applied to nearly all the purposes for which a single-acting engine could be used. The path had been opened by Worcester, laid out by Savery and his contemporaries, and the builders of the Newcomen engine followed it as far as they were able. Smeaton's contribution is often overlooked or undervalued because he didn't actually invent a new type of engine, but he did contribute as much to the development of the steam engine as any one of the inventors. Unrivalled as a mechanic and head and shoulders above any other engineer of his time, he was often visited by foreign engineers who sought advice with regard to work on the continent.

However, the engines I've described so far were only the beginning; all of these early developments just paved the way for the man who is regarded as the 'father of steam'. Those who had come before him are often simply referred to as 'Watt's predecessors'. But this description really does not do them justice. These men were either scientific explorers interested in experiments with steam, or more practical men who were looking for ways to meet one of the major challenges of their time, which was pumping water out of flooded coal or metal mines. Then came the challenge of harnessing power to every kind of machine. The progress of mechanization in the eighteenth century generated a demand for power on an unprecedented scale.

But cometh the hour and cometh the man, and James Watt came along just at the right time. He was born in Greenock, Scotland, in 1736, the son of a tradesman in the town who did a variety of work. As well as carpentry of all kinds, he was a shipwright and nautical instrument maker. Young James was a sickly lad and this, combined with the fact that he was very sensitive and shy, meant that he was never able to go to school, so his parents, who were respectable and intelligent people, educated him. He also spent a lot of time messing with his father's tools in the workshop, which helped him a great deal in later life. Yet he was a man born before his time and he is worthy of the credit he is given as the inventor of the modern steam engine.

There is a tale that James Watt realized how much potential steam had as a source of power while he was watching the lid of a boiling kettle when he was quite a young boy. Another story is that his auntie was always telling him off for wasting his time by taking off and putting on the lid of a kettle, holding saucers and spoons over the spout, watching the lid jumping up and down when it was boiling and catching the drops of water that were caused when the steam condensed. If nothing else, these stories are a good illustration of his powers of observation. Whether they are true or not we don't really know, but what is certain is that, when he was a little older, he did carry out experiments in Glasgow using a kettle as a small boiler.

At the age of eighteen, Watt went to Glasgow to work as an apprentice to a mathematical instrument maker. He had an enquiring mind and developed an interest in steam engines. When, in 1763, he was given a small model of a Newcomen engine to repair, he took the opportunity to have a good look at it and he realized how inefficient it was. He began to take great interest in the thing and went about getting patents on how he could improve it. He found that the Newcomen engine used up so much steam that it couldn't run for more than a few strokes at a time. It became clear to him that steam was wasted by the continual heating, cooling and reheating of the metal as first steam and then cold water to condense it, introduced to the cylinder. He saw the need to take greater care to economize on the steam, so he went about making careful calculations to minimize the loss of heat.

The breakthrough came to him as he was taking a walk one fine sunny morning. Watt realized that to keep the cylinder hot he would have to have a separate condenser – that is, another cylinder to condense the steam in so that the main cylinder would be able to stay hot all the time instead of being cooled at every stroke with the cold water. This was the most vital improvement that Watt made to Newcomen's invention, resulting in an immensely more powerful engine that saved roughly 75 per cent of the coal it burned. The inventor applied for and was granted a patent in 1769. For its time Watt's engine was a very complex thing; much better finished than Newcomen's, which was basically an iron pipe with a piston and old rope for the piston rings. Watt's had got to be made very precisely. The cylinders had to be cast with a degree of precision and they had to be bored and all the connecting rods had to be made to precise lengths and measurements. So it was a much more complicated thing and a bit beyond the style of the local village blacksmith or 'craftsman'.

One of the biggest problems Watt had in his early days was that, although he had the ideas, he had no money to spend on developing his engines or, more importantly, marketing them. In fact he fell into debt straight away attempting to market them, and his financial straits were made even more perilous by the endless patent litigation, which seemed to plague every British inventor of the day. Watt came close to bankruptcy so, as has always been the case, the man with the ideas had to find the men with the money to back him so that he could start manufacturing his steam engines. The two men who offered financial support and made possible the successful development of his steam engine were, first of all, John Roebuck and then Matthew Boulton,

John Roebuck was born in Sheffield in 1718 and he became quite a wealthy physician before he decided he fancied iron-making more than being a surgeon. He built a blast furnace on the River Carron in Stirlingshire, where there was plenty of water power, ready transport by sea and an abundant supply of coal, iron ore and limestone (all three components react together with air to create liquid iron and liquid slag). The first furnace was blown at Carron in 1760; and the first steam engine to work the blowing machinery of a blast furnace was erected at the Carron iron works in 1765.

The pits that Roebuck owned to provide the fuel for his iron-making activities were situated at Kinneil near Falkirk and he soon discovered to his cost that he had to make sure they were kept clear of water. He realized that to do this he was in need of a great pumping engine. Watt had already started on drawings for a similar machine and in 1769 he was given the order to build a pumping engine that would pump Roebuck's pits dry. Roebuck took on a £1,000 debt that Watt had built up during the development of this engine and helped him out with more finances in return for two thirds of Watt's patent. But Watt's engine was not ready for pumping the colliery for a long time and Roebuck, too, began to find himself in financial difficulties.

Roebuck couldn't find any more money for Watt's experiments and he also owed a considerable sum of money to Matthew Boulton, the owner of the Soho Ironworks in Birmingham. Boulton offered to take

Roebuck's share in Watt's engine as full settlement of the debt, rather than file a claim against him. So Boulton acquired two thirds of the engine patent in exchange for the remission of a debt of £630 and a further payment of £1,000. Ironically Roebuck's financial difficulties were further compounded by the fact that none of his creditors 'valued the engine at a farthing'!

Matthew Boulton was the son of a Birmingham silver stamper and piercer. He succeeded to his father's business and built up a great and very profitable establishment. He wasn't just a businessman, though; he was also a very clever man and he won the praise of Watt as a person of great ingenuity and foresight. With Roebuck now off the scene, Boulton soon obtained the full patent of Watt's steam engine and the partnership of Boulton and Watt was born. Watt left Scotland to live in England and he brought with him the engine that he had designed for the Kinneil mines. This was re-erected at Boulton's Soho Ironworks, where it was used to pump water to drive a waterwheel that powered the works. In the early days of steam this became quite common – steam and water being used together to run mills, factories and early engineering works.

Boulton and Watt became a great force in engineering. In 1775 Watt obtained an extension of his patent for twenty-five years and entered into partnership with Boulton for the same period. The object of the partnership was to supply and erect Watt's engine. The firm of Boulton and Watt grew into one of the most important industrial enterprises of the eighteenth century: they were a pioneering engineering firm which, for a period of twenty-five years, had the sole rights on steam power in Great Britain. It was in fact the union of one of the most inventive brains of the age with one of the first great commercial intelligences, for the purpose of selling one of the most valuable things in existence – power!

With his financial backing secure, it wasn't very long before Watt succeeded in producing a satisfactory engine. In fact, by 1776, two of his engines had been successfully installed – one for draining a coal mine at Tipton in Staffordshire and another to supply air for a blast furnace near Broseley in Shropshire. These two engines aroused great interest and soon orders were coming in to the Soho works.

At this stage a third figure arrived on the scene. William Murdock was another Scot, born in Ayrshire. His father was a millwright and William had considerable mechanical skill. In 1777 he came to the Soho works in search of employment and Boulton took him on to superintend the erection of the firm's engines in Cornwall, where they were being taken up in large numbers for pumping water from the tin and copper mines.

The engine business was well under way as regards orders, but Boulton, like Roebuck before him, was also to face a financial crisis. He had speculated in other interests indirectly linked with engines, and over-production at a time of depression in 1787, resulted in the insolvency of several firms. Boulton badly needed an extension of credit. He appealed to Watt, but Watt, with characteristic caution, had already safely invested his money, and the appeal was made in vain.

Remember that Boulton had, throughout the many hard years of struggle, taken all the financial risks and worries on his own shoulders. He had paid Watt a regular salary when the company was not making any money and, out of pure generosity, allowed him half the profits, instead of the agreed one third. When profits did begin to come in, Watt's action at this crisis appears mean and ungrateful. While Boulton weathered the storm and never again had his prosperity in doubt, it appears that Watt's struggles with money or, rather lack of it, when setting out with his engine design had made him very miserly.

The development of the Boulton and Watt steam engine brought along with it a lot of new techniques in machine design and manufacture. Until this time the blacksmith had shaped his iron work by eye, just working out dimensions as he banged away on his anvil. Boulton and Watt determined the dimensions and working parts of their engines in advance of production through the use of measured architectural-style drawings. This was a major advance in the design and manufacture of machinery. They had their engine parts machined, unlike Newcomen who blacksmithed his iron in the old way and bolted great baulks of wood together with big square-headed nuts and bolts. Newcomen's engines were a little primitive-looking and actually had a lot of woodwork in them, but Watt's bordered on the ornate and were quite beautiful if you look at the end product.

Really it was the beginning of a new age. Drawings not only permitted greater flexibility and precision in design (granting the tolerances of the day were very generous), but they also enabled production by division of labour. Engine parts could be drawn and designed in one place, manufactured in Birmingham and then shipped all the way down to Cornwall to be assembled. The men stood there assembling them from precise drawings rather than determining the dimensions by eye as blacksmiths had done previously. As well as this, calculations had to be made to construct the drawings, and further calculations could be made using the dimensions of the drawings to provide rough predictions of power or performance. Neither the use of drawings and mathematics, nor the new methods of metal-working had any place in the practice of the traditional blacksmith. As a result, the steam engine called for a new kind of practitioner, whose skills were far from common.

One of Watt's earliest engines can be seen in the Science Museum in London. *Old Bess* is a single-acting pumping engine. Built in 1777, it was the second engine to be produced at the Soho works. But it was the first to try the principle of the expansive working of steam. Watt's original system was to allow steam at boiler pressure to follow the piston throughout its stroke. Then he realized that if an admission valve was shut part-way through the stroke, and steam allowed to expand for the rest of the stroke, the steam could be used more economically, although the power output of the engine was reduced. With expansive working, the action of the engine was irregular and hard to control and it became known as *Beelzebub*. *Old Bess* was built as a returning engine, to lift water from the kill race (the channel that carries water from the waterwheel) and return it to the launder (a wooden trough that carries water from the millstream to the top of the waterwheel). It was a common engine for obtaining rotative motion where a natural stream didn't exist.

But the biggest breakthrough was still to come. An engine like *Old Bess* was basically still a pumping engine, which was used to raise water for a waterwheel. It was the waterwheel rather than the engine that provided the rotative power to drive the machinery in a factory. Until an effective rotative steam engine, which could turn a lineshaft, was invented, early steam engines, including Watt's, could do nothing but pump water. However, with changing economic demands, largely due to the introduction of new machinery into the textiles industry, there also needed to be a change in the type of engines that were made to power this machinery.

One of the pioneers was John Stewart, who wanted to use steam power in sugar-cane mills in the West Indies. He introduced an engine, but it proved a failure because he couldn't find a way of using the power that was generated to turn a shaft, which would turn the workings of the machines. Matthew Boulton realized that there was a need for alternative forms of power like a rotative engine or one that would turn wheels round to drive machines in factories, and he

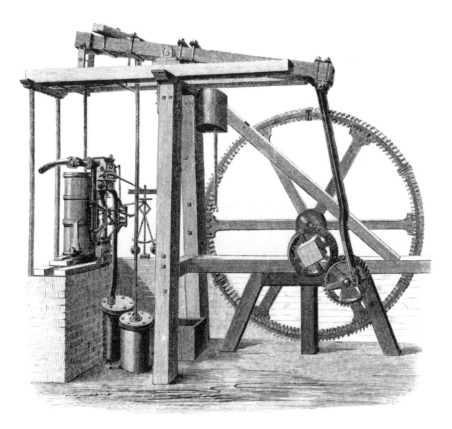

Above: An engraving of *Old Bess* designed by James Watt and the first engine to give rotary rather than pumping motion. It was also an improvement on Newcomen's engines as the steam condensed in a separate vessel rather than within the cylinder.

pressed Watt to develop one. He had to find some way of converting the oscillating motion of the steam engine beam to rotative action. Boulton and Watt were not the first to build rotative engines, but theirs were the best. Only they could use Watt's patented separate condenser; the vital improvement that made Watt's engines three times as economical in fuel as all the others.

The breakthrough in converting reciprocating engines to rotative motion by mechanical means came in the 1780s, headed by Watt. He made an engine double-acting by applying steam alternately below and above the piston to produce a power stroke in both directions. Simultaneously, a number of other engineers introduced their own rotative engines and I think they had a bit of an argy-bargy over the crank. One of these was James Pickard, who adopted a crank and flywheel in his engine.

This forced Watt to think along different lines and in 1781 he introduced what he described as his 'sun and planet gear'. In this, the sun wheel was fixed to the flywheel shaft and the planet wheel to the connecting rod, which was hung from the beam. The rocking of the beam turned the planet wheel, which then turned the sun wheel and this rotated a shaft. This was the beginning of the beam engine that most people know – with a cylinder at one end, a beam across the top, the crank at the other end and the flywheel.

It was this that led to Watt's big breakthrough when, three years later, he came up with his idea of 'parallel motion', an ingenious device for transferring power from the rocking movement of the engine beam to the vertical motion of the pump rod. The device was necessary because a piston can operate only on a vertical axis, while the motion of the beam runs along a curve. Watt's invention was a parallelogram of jointed rods fixed on the underside of the beam, with one angle fastened to the head of the piston rod. The whole contraption is carried through the curve described by the end of the beam, while allowing the piston rod driving the beam, to stay on its vertical axis. Watt's device was actually a sort of hinge, which pivoted in two places. As the piston rod went up and down, the hinge bent and the whole thing kept the piston rod in a true parallel plane with the cylinder. By 1784 he was able to supply engines capable of 'giving motion to the wheels of industry'. Watt now began thinking in terms of horsepower and his engines were referred to as 14-horse engines, or 20-horse engines and so on. As well as the development of parallel motion and the separate condenser, other improvements that Watt made included lagging the cylinder and inventing a governor to regulate the speed of the engine. The design used the expansive properties of steam, where the steam is admitted for only part of the stroke of the piston, and the expansion of the steam does the rest of the work.

The Boulton and Watt engine was fully developed by 1787. It satisfied a large part of the increasing demand for power until 1800, when Watt's patent for the separate condenser expired. During this period the firm supplied nearly 300 rotative engines. The rotative steam engine was the first source of power that could be applied on a large scale to drive any type of machine, anywhere, at any time, needing only to be supplied with fuel and cold water. It set industry free from reliance on water, wind or animal power and so made industrial expansion possible.

The popular belief has always been that Watt was the inventor of the steam engine, but that's not really the case. What he did was to make something that was already in existence more efficient. His machinery was much, much better than anything that had been around up to that time. Watt alone had turned what was basically just a steam pump into a very efficient machine, which drove the Industrial Revolution. As early as 1787 its adaptability to various uses was described as almost incredible, while the *European Magazine* stated that it would 'change the appearance of the civilized world', as indeed it did. We could produce iron and steel and textiles, and of course the ordinary worker's life would never be the same again – we'd all become enslaved by steam engines. The engines reigned on in basically the same form as Watt designed them throughout the nineteenth century and well into the twentieth. Right up until around 1947 in Bolton there were great beam engines still driving a cotton mill. And it was very impressive to watch one work.

James Watt might be regarded as the father of the steam engine, but the greatest advances were made by Richard Trevithick in the 1790s and early 1800s. Trevithick was a brilliant mechanical engineer and inventor, who has not always been given full credit for his inventions and for the contribution he made to the development of steam power in mines and factories and for road, rail and marine transport. All through his career Trevithick remained barely literate, but he showed an extraordinary talent in engineering with an intuitive ability to solve problems that puzzled much more educated engineers. He was a colourful character, short-tempered and famed for his great strength. Unfortunately, though, he was totally lacking in any business sense. In spite of this, in an eventful career, which included making and losing a fortune in the silver mines of South America, he was the first in the field with many of the major developments in steam power.

Richard Trevithick was born at Redruth in Cornwall on 13 April 1771, the fifth child and only son of the manager of the Wheal Chance copper mine near Camborne. When he was a youth he lived at Illogan in the tin-mining district of Cornwall and attended the village school, but more often than not he played truant. When he did manage to get to school the headmaster said he was disobedient, inattentive and a bit of a waster. I suppose his school report would have been rather like mine: 'could try harder' and all that. His father didn't think much better of him either and referred to him as a loafer.

Even at this time Trevithick was much more interested in the engines in the mines that surrounded him than in his school work, and he spent a lot of his boyhood wandering the countryside looking at the mines. No doubt that's where he got his first inspiration to be a mechanical man. It was at this early age that he amazed those who had a better education than him by solving problems through his own intuition rather than by applying theory to them. He had a wonderfully inventive mind. His other asset was that he was a great big fellow and he earned a bit of money doing bare-knuckle fighting and wrestling.

Trevithick's father, seeing that his son's interest was in machinery, apprenticed him to William Murdock, who worked for James Watt. At this time Murdock was managing the building of pumping engines in Cornwall. I rather think that Trevithick must have learned all the 'noble arts', like working whatever type of lathe they had and drilling machines and planing machines. I believe that's where he learned all his skills. Of course when you serve as an apprentice that's what you're there for, to learn how to do the job.

Trevithick's great dream was to design an engine that worked on high-pressure steam, or what he called 'strong steam'. James Watt had always refused to use high-pressure steam because of the dangers involved. He believed that the boiler would explode, mainly because the materials that were available for making boilers then weren't strong enough to withstand the great pressure. One of the problems was the quality of the wrought-iron plates, which couldn't be made very big. Cast iron was quite commonly used at the time. His first locomotive had a cast-iron boiler, which is a recipe for disaster: if you get too much steam in it, and with no safety valve you're asking for big trouble.

But Trevithick was a wilder man than Watt, and even though he was very aware of the danger, he realized that such an engine would be much lighter than anything Boulton and Watt had built and this would open up new commercial possibilities. So Trevithick started the dangerous business of conducting experiments with high-pressure steam and brought about huge improvements to the old Watt engines through his amazing grasp of its principles and use. At this time and right on until almost the middle of the nineteenth century, most steam engines were still based on the design principles of those of Boulton and Watt – they were basically beam engines with a vertical cylinder under one end of the beam and a crank under the other. They worked in the same way as low-pressure condensing engines, powered by a vacuum, which was created by condensation of low-pressure steam. But from around the 1790s these engines started to be overtaken by new designs.

I suppose that Murdock and Trevithick talked about steam engines all day long. As well as being James Watt's man in Cornwall, Murdock was quite famous for producing a lovely model of an early steam carriage, and Trevithick soon started making models himself. The first and earliest ones were of mine-pumping engines, which worked on the principle of high pressure. As far back as 1796 Trevithick made models of steam locomotives, which he ran round the table at home to show his friends. He poured hot water into the boiler and put a red-hot iron into a tube beneath, which raised steam and set the engine in motion. One of his most interesting models can be seen at the Science Museum in London – a perfect specimen of a high-pressure engine. His engines became known as 'non-condensing' because they didn't use the principle of condensing steam to create a vacuum into which the piston would move; instead Trevithick used the power derived from the compression of high-pressure steam. The principle of using steam at high pressure to drive the piston was already well known, but it took the boldness of Trevithick to overcome the engineering difficulties. With the water at super-hot temperatures the boiler could easily have blown up, so good materials and good seals were needed. His engines worked very well but they were three times less economical than Watt's atmospheric engines, which were quite gentle, using the expansive properties of the steam, condensing it with water and creating a vacuum, against the atmosphere – hence the economy that the Watt engine had compared with Trevithick's high-pressure one. But although Trevithick's engine was less efficient than earlier models, it was much more compact, and it was this that made steam locomotive practicable.

The Darby Ironworks at Coalbrookdale in Shropshire is known as the cradle of the Industrial Revolution because it was here that Abraham Darby set up the first big smelting operation able to produce iron in large quantities. And it was after a series of visits that Trevithick made to Coalbrookdale in the 1790s that he constructed his first high-pressure engine for winding ore, in 1798. The engine was used for powering a winding machine to raise loads of iron ore from the mines, up the mineshaft, to the surface. The engines that he built for the tin mines used a cross beam to work a pump. He experimented with what was almost a reckless abandon and disregard for any dangers, using hitherto unheard-of pressures of up to 100 lbs per square inch (7 kg per cm²). Crucial to the success of Trevithick's engine was the breakthrough that he made in boiler design. His large wrought-iron boiler, with its single internal flue, became known throughout the world as the 'Cornish boiler'.

Before his invention of the Cornish boiler most boilers were shaped like American Wild West wagons and, not surprisingly, were known as 'wagon boilers'. They consisted of a big horseshoe-shaped wrapper with a concave bottom and two brick walls and a fire underneath it – in other words, they were like big kettles. The trouble with these was that all the sediment in the water settled on the bottom and, like the bottom of an old kettle, it all got encrusted. The fire had a devastating effect on the plates and there were many explosions. Trevithick's Cornish boiler was totally different. It had one great fire tube from end to end through the outer shell and the fire was in there, so the products of combustion went straight up the middle. As a result it boiled the water nicely and then the heat went down and along the bottom, turned round two corners and went back along the sides of the boiler. So not only did the boiler have a fire inside it, it had one outside on either side as well. This proved to be the best and most economical boiler during the early 1800s.

Although many of Trevithick's early engines were made to pump water from the Cornish tin and copper mines, they had many other uses too. In fact, one of the world's first engines to operate with the steam produced at a high pressure was installed by Trevithick to drive the machinery of a dye house at Lambeth in London. The great boiler was 6 feet (1.8 m) in diameter and was originally made from cast iron. It was cast at Abraham Darby's foundry in Coalbrookdale and it had a double-acting cylinder, which was 8 inches (20.3 cm) in diameter with a working stroke of 48 inches (1.2 m). The engine was rated at 6 horsepower (4.5 kw) and it made twenty-four revolutions per minute, with a boiler pressure of 45 lbs per square inch (3 kg per cm^2).

Trevithick's engines consumed three times as much coal as Watt's, but they were compact, simple and easy to install. They didn't need the great volume of cold water that was required by condensing engines. With the progress made by Trevithick, Watt now found himself in an increasingly difficult position. He was still convinced that this move towards greater power and efficiency in steam engines also posed a serious problem of explosion. But there wasn't much that Boulton and Watt could do to slow down the economic and industrial forces, which were demanding greater and greater power from the steam engine. If they refused to develop the required technology, others would certainly be willing to take up the dangerous challenge of high-pressure steam. In the end Watt did refuse to make high-pressure engines, fearing that he could not make the boiler and the engine strong enough to withstand such pressure. He used his influence to slow the development of the high-pressure engine and alert the public to the dangers and other engineers to their responsibilities concerning safety. He was so active in campaigning against the use of high-pressure steam that Trevithick complained that Boulton and Watt were exaggerating the risks involved. In spite of Watt's resistance, however, Trevithick's high-pressure steam was soon to win the day. But that is not his greatest claim to fame. It is as the first engineer to apply steam power to the haulage of loads on a railway that Trevithick made his greatest contribution to technology.

CHAPTER TWO

THE TRANSPORT REVOLUTION

I was born in a collection of terraced houses, similar to those in television's *Coronation Street*, all clustered together. As a little lad I could stand at the back-bedroom window and look down an alleyway, up another long back street and see the signal box on the main railway line from Manchester through Bolton. It was magnificent; on a moonlit night you could hear the whistle sound as the locomotive was approaching. It would bash across the end of the ginnel (alley) with the fire-hole door open. There would be a big shaft of fire in the sky and you could see two characters on the footplate crouched in position. Without a shadow of a doubt, that's what really inspired me and got me interested in steam engines.

Not very far away there were the engine sheds. On my way home from school I used to do a little detour to look through the gates, and occasionally I got brave and ventured in. In those days you had a bit more respect for authority and you didn't go trespassing, as you might say. Later on in my life a lot of my relations worked on the railway. The railway company owned rows of housing near Burnden Park football ground, where Bolton Wanderers used to play, where all the engine drivers and firemen lived. When I got to the boozing age of about fifteen or sixteen and was in the pub for the first time, I used to talk to the engine drivers. Then I got really lucky. I used to sit on the end of the platform at night with a penny platform ticket in the pouring rain and a driver would come in with a locomotive and stop it dead level with me at the end of the platform. He'd take a quick look up and down to see if there was anybody important about and then give me a wave to run and jump on the engine. Then we went 20 miles (32 km) through the night – in the days of gaslight (this was the

1950s) it was quite exciting. I remember him saying to me, 'Don't let go of the shovel into the fire box or we're done for.' It's amazing really when you think that just one shovel makes a great locomotive and hundreds of tons of carriages actually move along.

There's a lot of enthusiasm now for the steam railways. It's a touch of 'when it's all gone, everybody wants one', I think. But there is something special about a steam locomotive. When it's steamed up, it comes to life and it smells fantastic, with the sulphur in the smoke. It's something that I don't think anybody can really put into words. To me, looking at a railway line now just isn't the same. All those stanchions and electric wires are terribly unsightly compared to two beautiful silver streaks through the fields, just posts and rail fences along each side and the odd signal sticking up. It looked a lot more picturesque in the old days and a lot more beautiful than it does now. I'm sure there could have been a better way than electricity; it's just cheap and convenient and doesn't cost as much as steam engines.

Steam power brought about a revolution in transport. It was one of Britain's great contributions to the world. When the railways first appeared at the beginning of the nineteenth century they changed the face of Britain. Great bridges and cuttings were built; materials and people could be moved from one end of the country to the other a lot more quickly than they could with horses and carriages. Even standard time was introduced with the coming of the railways. Previously people had set their clocks to sunset, so if sunset happened at 8 pm in London, it was 20 minutes later in Penzance when the sun went down, and it was 8 pm there.

When people think of railway locomotives, they usually picture great, powerful engines like the *Flying Scotsman*. But a loco like this represents the peak of steam locomotive engineering. To tell the story of how it all began we have to go back to Richard Trevithick and his construction of the world's first steam railway locomotive between 1803 and 1804. Although he wasn't the world's greatest businessman, Trevithick was a visionary and had already shown that he was very aware of the commercial possibilities of developing the steam engine. The greatest of these that he identified was finding a way to use the steam engine for transportation. And it was the invention of a relatively small, high-pressure, stationary engine for pumping mines that made the locomotive possible. Around this time Napoleon's conquests in Europe had caused the price of animal feed to rocket, so why not, reasoned Trevithick, replace live horses with an 'iron horse' – one that mine owners could feed with their own coal?

Above: An early sketch showing Newton's idea for a boiler mounted on a carriage.

The very first scheme for applying steam to locomotion was probably that of the illustrious Sir Isaac Newton, who in 1680 proposed a machine which consisted of a spherical boiler mounted on a carriage. But it was not until the end of the eighteenth century, when the stationary steam engine had become so well developed, that the possibility of its successful application to locomotion began to be fully recognized, and it was at this time that many inventors tried to tackle the problem.

A French army officer, Nicholas Joseph Cugnot, made the first experiment in 1769. A very talented mechanic, he was born in Vaud, Lorraine in 1725 and served in both the French and German armies. He built a steam carriage to transport artillery, which was set at work in the presence of the French minister of war. The engine consisted of two beams of heavy timber extending from end to end supported by two strong wheels behind and one heavier but smaller wheel in front. The single wheel was turned by two single-acting engines, one on each side, supplied with steam from a boiler suspended in front of the machine. The driver steered the machine by a gearing system, which turned the whole frame. It was found to be a good plan, but the boiler was too small and the steering apparatus too slow. Unfortunately Cugnot's experiments were brought to an untimely end by the death of one of his patrons and the exile of another. But he had proved that it was possible to move a vehicle by its own steam.

Back in England, James Watt was concentrating his inventive mind on the problem. He wanted to apply his engine to locomotion, using either a non-condensing engine or an air-surface condenser. He included the locomotive engine in his patent of 1784 and his assistant, Murdock, made a working locomotive. It is said to have run at 6 to 8 miles an hour (10-13 kmph). It was after seeing a model engine constructed by Murdock that Trevithick, who was his pupil at this time, decided that he was going to build a carriage that would run on common roads. He was joined in the enterprise by Andrew Vivian.

In partnership with Vivian, Trevithick started to build his first road locomotive at Camborne in November 1800. He employed several workmen to repair and improve his mining engines and pumping machinery and they spent their spare time putting the little locomotive together. The engine, which he called *The Puffing Devil*, was a mixture of wood and iron, all blacksmith-made, but it worked. The locomotive was extremely simple compared with other engines of that time – Trevithick discarded improvements made by Watt, such as the air pump, condenser and parallel motion. Apparently the only drawback was that the boiler was too small and the steam couldn't be kept up for long when the locomotive was on its way. The steam carriage looked like a stagecoach, and it was built on four wheels. It had one horizontal cylinder and this, together with the boiler and furnace-box, was placed in the rear of the back axle. The motion of the piston was transmitted to a separate crank-axle and it was from this that the axle of the driving wheel got its motion. The steam-racks and force pumps and the bellows used in generating combustion were worked off the same crank-axle. It was the first successful high-pressure engine constructed on the principle of a moving piston, which was not only raised but also depressed by the steam.

The engine was ready for testing on Christmas Eve, 1801. When Trevithick started to turn on the steam, seven or eight people jumped on and this strange-looking vehicle set off up the hill at Camborne faster than walking pace. The story goes that when they got to the top of the hill they went into an inn and did some celebrating. While they were in there they left the engine outside and, unfortunately, it burnt out. However, a reproduction of this locomotive has recently been made and it actually works. They tell me that Camborne hill is not the hill that it used to be, but the engine still went up that hill. Trevithick had made the first road locomotive, which carried passengers on the English highway. It was leaps and bounds ahead of the carriage Cugnot had made that carried passengers in Paris just thirty years earlier.

Trevithick's only problem was lack of funds: he couldn't afford to continue running the carriages at his own expense.

In the following year Trevithick took out a patent for a passenger-carrying steam road carriage. This was assembled at Felton's carriage-works in Leather Lane, London. On completion, the *London Steam Carriage* was driven about 10 miles (16 km) through the streets of London to Paddington and back through Islington with seven or eight guest passengers. This was the first trip of a self-powered passenger-carrying vehicle in the world. It must have been quite a sight at the time. However, disaster struck once again when Trevithick and his colleague crashed the carriage into some house railings.

The *London Steam Carriage* was an incredibly ponderous machine with massive wheels, which were about 7 feet (2.1 m) in diameter at the back. It needed to be strong because of the state of the roads at the time – there were big boulders and stones everywhere and deep ruts cut by the narrow wheels of horse-drawn carriages. A man living near Macclesfield has actually reconstructed one of these engines from the drawings that still exist. They're not very detailed drawings, so a bit of guesswork has been involved in interpreting them. I've seen this machine at Macclesfield run and it's just like it's described in the history books, a very ponderous piece of tackle. The wheels are so large and of such a narrow gauge that on a grass field it's very unstable. On a good tarmac road, though, it's beautiful.

Back in 1803 Trevithick built a second carriage, which he later drove through the streets of London. It was driven by its own steam, 90 miles (145 km) from Camborne to Plymouth, and then shipped by water. Ultimately, however, the project to build a steam-powered passenger-carrying vehicle was not a success for Trevithick. It was too expensive and it needed two men and a bag of coal to what one man and a bag of hay could do with a horse-drawn vehicle. In the end the coach was removed and the engine sold for driving a hoop-rolling mill.

Trevithick's main difficulty had been lack of funds; he couldn't afford to continue running the carriages at his own expense. And there was another, even greater problem. Although he had a reasonable amount of success running this kind of carriage on common roads, it soon became obvious that the roads in England were too rough and uneven for the successful use of such machines, and he abandoned his steam carriage as a practical failure.

But these early locomotives of Trevithick's started off the whole development of road transport. As with all good inventions, news of them soon spread and it wasn't very long before everybody was having a go at making steam carriages. Various companies were set up and steam buses or steam stagecoaches steamed around everywhere. From the etchings and the drawings made at the time, you can see that they were very ponderous and probably quite dangerous. And of course the turnpike-road people and those who ran stagecoaches got quite jealous and committed acts of sabotage, like throwing rocks in the vehicles' paths.

Another drawback of the very early road locomotives was that the braking system wasn't that good. You can imagine one of the large-diameter wheels hitting a rock and just disintegrating, and all the passengers being parachuted into space. A lot of the engines had only three wheels, so would have been very unstable. The efforts that went into developing steam carriages must have been held back because of the state of the roads. They were so bad at the beginning of the nineteenth century that people reverted back to using horse and carriage again. My impression is that if British roads had not been so poor in the early nineteenth century, the early history of road transport would have been quite different.

Trevithick had spent nearly three years on his experiments, and they had emptied his pockets and those of his partner, Andrew Vivian. But he didn't give up the idea of applying steam power to locomotion and it was probably because of the state of the roads that he turned his attention to developing a steam carriage locomotive to run upon the tram roads: horse-worked railways used all over the mining districts in England that were by now in general use throughout Britain. In 1804 he started to build a small locomotive for a south Wales iron and mining business that he called the *Pen y Darren*. The design was based on a compact stationary engine/boiler that he had developed, and it was completed and tested within the same year. The boiler was cylindrical in form, flat at the ends and it was made of cast iron. The furnace and flues were inside the boiler, in which a single cylinder of

8 inches (20 cm) in diameter and 4-feet-6-inch (1.35 m) was immersed upright. The *Pen y Darren* pulled a load of 10 tons of iron ore and seventy men along a track at the Merthyr Tydfil Colliery in south Wales and it did 5 miles an hour (8 kmph) for all of 10 miles (16 km), which of course in those days was an unbelievable achievement. The engine won Trevithick a £500 bet for being the first man in the world to build a locomotive. This was a long time before George Stephenson and the men in the north east.

Despite this initial success, however, the railway was abandoned as a failure. But it can be seen as the first attempt to adapt the steam engine to work on a railroad. The track on which Trevithick ran the locomotive had been a horse-drawn tramway, which had been built to transport iron to the Glamorganshire Canal. The great problem of the time, of course, was the quality of the materials. The rails on which the locomotive ran were made of cast iron and short; the engine was fairly heavy. The vibrations and the thumping of the iron wheels on the rails proved too much and there were many, many failures where the rails broke. The whole project was slowly but surely abandoned – it was the same story with the road carriage or the steam stagecoach. The state of the roads let the road carriage down and the quality of the cast iron let the railway engine down. There needed to be advances in rail technology – new materials of wrought iron and later steel and different shapes: rolled iron with the flange taken off the rails and put on the train wheels.

Trevithick built a second locomotive at Gateshead in 1805 and in 1808 he demonstrated a third on a circular track laid near Euston Road in London. On 21 February 1808, one of the most significant dates in railway history, he put to work a steam carriage called *Catch Me Who Can* – which almost anybody could do, because it moved little faster than walking pace. He displayed it in London in 1808 behind a closed circular fence. Passengers could ride the circuit for a shilling a time in an attached road coach refitted with special wheels. Admission cards for the event carried the impressive motto: 'Mechanical power subduing animal speed'. The engine was a very plain and simple affair, weighing about 10 tons. The steam-cylinder was set vertically in the after-end of the boiler, and the crosshead was connected to two rods, one on either

TREVITHICKS,
PORTABLE STEAM ENGINE

Catch me who can.

Mechanical Power Subduing
Animal Speed.

Above: An advertisement for Trevithick's *Catch me who can.*

side, driving the pair of wheels at the back. The exhaust steam entered the chimney, aiding the draught. Eventually the engine was thrown from the track because of a break in the rail and, because all of Trevithick's funds had been spent, it was never replaced. He then abandoned these projects because it was clear that cast-iron rails were too brittle for the weight of his engines. But his achievement of hauling a load of 10 tons of iron and seventy men along ten miles (16 km) of tramway gives him a claim to being the real 'father of the railways' rather than George Stephenson. Trevithick could certainly be regarded as the 'father of the locomotive'. Another of his engines, *Black Billy*, went to Tyneside and proved to be the inspiration for a young enginewright there, George Stephenson. But that was over twenty years later, and in the meantime other engineers had a go at building a railway and designing a locomotive that would run along rails.

In the beginning, though, they had a lot of bother. The main problem that faced Trevithick and all the early engineers was the cast-iron rails: they couldn't find enough grip. For a long time it was believed that a smooth steel locomotive wheel on a smooth rail would skid and wouldn't be able to pull a load. There were various schools of thought regarding the track and engineers tried different ways of solving the problem. One of the first was John Blenkinsop, who went to Leeds to construct a locomotive to run on a track at Middleton. Like all the early railways it was built to transport coal from the mines down to the river or the sea – in this case the River Aire in the centre of Leeds. In 1811 Blenkinsop took out a patent for a rack-and-pinion form of propulsion for his steam locomotives. The idea was to have a cogged wheel attached to the side of the engine, which would pull it along by engaging in teeth cast into the side of the rails. The boiler of his engine was supported by a four-wheel carriage, which was independent of the working parts of the engine.

In 1812 this engine began running on the railway from the Middleton collieries to the centre of Leeds, a distance of about 3¼ miles (5.2 km). Six or seven locomotives in all were constructed to his design and they pulled thirty fully loaded coal wagons at a speed of 3¼ miles per hour (5.2 kmph). They were in use for many years, and although other railways, which came later, have become more famous, the Middleton railway was the first place where locomotive power was used on a railway line on a regular basis for commercial purposes.

The Middleton railway gave great impetus to the growth of Leeds and the city's industries. It made possible a good supply of cheap coal, which was of benefit to the developing use of steam engines in textile mills and other factories. Its pioneering use of steam locomotives proved to the world that they were commercially viable and led to the development of an extensive locomotive-building industry in Leeds.

At first everybody thought that the rack-and-pinion system that had been used in Leeds was the way to do it. But it wasn't very long before they discovered that a smooth steel wheel would get traction on a smooth iron rail. And, although the Middleton railway can claim to be the first regularly operated steam railway in the world, it is to Northumbria that we have to go to find the 'great men' of the railways, the men who were the pioneers of steel and steam. Three of them were born within a few miles of each other: William Hedley at Newburn, and Timothy Hackworth and George Stephenson at Wylam. All three of them were involved with the region's expanding coal industry.

William Hedley was colliery manager at Wylam Colliery in Northumberland and Christopher Blackett was the owner. Blackett had been interested in using locomotives for a long time and, as early as 1804, he had employed Trevithick to build a locomotive engine to replace horse-drawn coal wagons. The locomotive was built, but there was a problem because it weighed 5 tons and was too heavy for Blackett's wooden wagonway. In 1808 Blackett replaced his wooden rails with cast-iron ones. He contacted Trevithick to supply another locomotive, but Trevithick was either unable or not inclined to build him one. Perhaps he'd not been paid for the first one. So in October 1812 Blackett asked Hedley to have a go at building a locomotive himself. Hedley was fortunate in that he had two very skilled craftsmen working at the pit who were able to help him: Jonathan Foster, an enginewright, and Timothy Hackworth, a blacksmith. The idea of using a rack-and-pinion system like the one in operation on the Middleton railway was looked into, but to convert the 5 miles (8 km) of smooth wrought-iron plateway that Blackett had already laid would have cost him £8,000, which was a considerable sum at that time. Anyway, Hedley had other ideas. He believed that if the wheels of the locomotive were coupled together, the weight of the locomotive alone would provide sufficient grip to haul a train of loaded wagons even where smooth wheels were running on smooth rails.

He set about building an engine with smooth wheels, and patented his design on 13 March 1813, a month after he had put his machine to work. The locomotive had a cast-iron boiler, and a single steam-cylinder 6 inches (15.2 cm) in diameter, with a small flywheel. The boiler of this engine was too small, so he had to build a bigger one with a return-flue boiler made of wrought iron. When Hedley's first engine was ready, the go-ahead was given, but the engine wouldn't move an inch. When it was finally set in motion, it flew to pieces, and the workmen and spectators, along with Blackett, the mine owner, scattered and fled in every direction! The machine, or what was left of it, was taken off the railway, and afterwards part of it was used as a pump at one of the mines.

Hedley's second engine wasn't much more successful. At first it pulled eight loaded coal-wagons at a speed of 5 miles per hour (8 kmph). A little later he managed to get the speed up to 10 miles an hour (16 kmph). Generally, though, it crept along at a snail's pace, sometimes taking six hours to cover the 5 miles (8 km) to the landing-place. It was continually dismounting the track and horses were needed to set it back on. The engine often broke down; its pumps, plugs and cranks would often not be the right ones; and the horses would again be needed, this time to take it back to the shop. Another problem at this time was that the rails still kept breaking under the weight of the locomotives. Until rails were made of wrought iron they could not be relied on. In fact, they became so unreliable that a horse was usually sent along with the locomotive just in case there was a disaster. In the very early days there was a lot of trial and error, but Hedley's engines continued in use at Wylam Colliery for many years.

The steam railway was essentially the result of two major technical advances: the ability to produce the necessary quantities of high-quality, low-cost, wrought-iron rails and the great advances that were being made at this time in steam-engine technology. The first steam locomotives built by Trevithick, Blenkinsop and Hedley all suffered from technical inadequacies. Low speeds of around 4 miles per hour (6.4 kmph), limited power and a tendency to break down on a regular basis meant that early locomotives weren't a serious alternative to road or canal transport. But in spite of these inadequacies, it was the work of pioneers like these three men that paved the way for George Stephenson.

Though there had been other locomotive builders before him, like Trevithick, George Stephenson is the man credited as the 'father of the railways'. He was active as an engine builder at about the time that Blenkinsop and Hedley started to build their engines and was already being talked about as a brilliant and ambitious engineer. Stephenson's great talent, though, was that he combined all the advantages of natural, inventive talent with an excellent mechanical training and entrepreneurial spirit. He was the first man to make and run a locomotive with flanged wheels on a track laid with cast-iron rails. His first engine, *Blucher* was built while he was working at Killingworth Colliery and ran in 1814. Stephenson's engines were remarkably well made and were referred to by one enthusiast as being 'superior beyond all comparison to all other engines ever seen'.

George Stephenson was born on 9 June 1781 in the small colliery village of Wylam on the north bank of the River Tyne near Newcastle. As a small boy he looked after the cows, but he wasn't destined to be a farmer because he had a strong mechanical bent and a great interest in steam machinery. His father worked at a local colliery and I suppose he would nip round there and have a look at the machines that made the pit work. While he was working as a herd-boy he used to keep himself amused by making clay models of engines, and it was soon realized that he had this wonderful mechanical talent. As he grew older he never lost an opportunity to learn about the construction and management of machinery. Later on he improved the work of others on steam engines and winding engines and eventually became interested in constructing locomotives.

The first job Stephenson had in the mines was a 'picker'. His duty was to clean the coal of stone, slate and other impurities. His starting wages was sixpence a day. At fifteen years of age he was promoted to the position of fireman. His attention to duty and his intelligence soon brought him further promotion, until, when he was still only seventeen years old, he was placed in charge of the pumping engine at Water Row pit, with his father working under him as fireman. In 1812 Stephenson was made enginewright at the Killingworth High Pit. By this time he was earning £100 a year, and one of his duties was to supervise the machinery of a group of collieries. It was while he was at Killingworth that he began a systematic course of self-improvement and first began to be recognized as an inventor of some note. His cottage was like a curiosity shop, filled with models of engines, machines of various kinds and interesting pieces of apparatus.

Stephenson was very aware of all that was going on at the time with regard to the development of the steam locomotive and he studied the design of all those that were around. He certainly took some of his ideas from Trevithick's work and, hearing of Hedley's work at Wylam, he went over to the colliery to study his engine. He also went to Leeds to see the Blenkinsop engine at its trials, when it pulled a load of 70 tons at a speed of 3¼ miles per hour (5.2 kmph). When he was there he expressed his opinion in the characteristic remark: 'I think I could make a better engine than that to go upon legs.' Very soon he was able to make an attempt. Once he'd seen the Blenkinsop and Hedley engines, Stephenson was determined to build his own, so he convinced Lord Ravensworth, the mine owner, of the advantages to be gained from using a travelling engine. Ravensworth advanced Stephenson the money that he needed and work started on his first locomotive engine in his workshops at West Moor.

This first engine, *Blucher*, proved to be defective, and the cost of using it was found to be about as great as that of using horsepower.

Stephenson was determined to build another engine, this time to a different plan, and he patented his new design in February 1815. It proved a much more efficient machine than *Blucher*. But this was only the start for Stephenson. It was this early work that set him on the path to becoming the most famous name in railway history. For many people, the world's railway history dates from 27 September 1825 when Stephenson drove his engine *Locomotion No.1* with its train of thirty-four vehicles along the 26 miles (42 km) of track that he had built between Stockton and Darlington. The weight of the train was 90 tons and it reached the phenomenal speed of 12 miles per hour (19 kmph)!

The Stockton and Darlington Railway was the first iron road built for public transport and the first to be used regularly by locomotive engines. The essential elements, a level course, metal rails on that course and locomotives to haul trains, combined with the genius of George Stephenson, brought about the greatest revolution in land transport the world had ever seen.

The story started in 1823, when Stephenson was made engineer of the Stockton and Darlington Railway. It was in this same year that his son, Robert, became director of the first locomotive factory in the world at only nineteen years of age when the Robert Stephenson and Company works was founded on South Street within the new industrial area around Forth Street in Newcastle upon Tyne. The building of the workshop, which went on to become one of the most famous establishments in the history of railways, was begun in 1824. The Stockton and Darlington line had been planned to transport coal from the Durham coalfields to the sea. Edward Pease, a Quaker industrialist from Darlington, was one of Stephenson's main backers and he was a big fan of the Killingworth engines and their work, and of the great advantages they would get from using them on the new line. He was so keen on getting steam locomotives to provide the power for the line that he not only supported Stephenson's argument, but also gave him an advance of £1,000 to help him to begin the business of locomotive-engine construction at Newcastle.

The honour of laying the first few lengths of rail in the presence of the mayor and other such dignitaries fell to Mr Meynell, the chairman of the Stockton and Darlington Railway Company. He made history when he spaced the rails 4 feet 8 inches (1.4 m) apart, which was merely a perpetuation of the distance between the wheels of road wagons. This width, which was slightly enlarged to 4 feet 8½ inches (1.41 m) to permit freer running, became the 'standard gauge' of railways in Britain. By the middle of 1825 all the track had been laid, and on a historic day in September of that year a train with a strange-looking engine in front and thirty-four wagons filled with passengers, flour and coal behind, steamed into history. The locomotive ran on four wheels, with a four-wheel tender to carry the coal and water. The driver had to balance precariously on a platform on the left-hand side of the engine, where he could control the supply of steam to the cylinders and operate the primitive valve gear. The fireman rode on the front of the tender, although when he was not stoking the fire he could ride on the platform on the opposite side of the engine to the driver. The engine, like many of the early locomotives, was not fitted with any brakes. On the opening day George Stephenson was the driver and he had two of his brothers as firemen.

On its way to Darlington the train frequently reached a speed of 12 miles per hour (19 kmph), and on one occasion it got up to 15 miles per hour (24 kmph). People on horseback and on foot tried to race the train as it passed triumphantly along. Spectators came out in their thousands to line the track, waving and cheering as this strange contraption went past. What a sight it must have been! When it reached Darlington it seemed that the whole town had turned out to see the train arrive, and then steam off towards Stockton, to arrive there in just over three hours. After the events of the opening day the railway had to settle down to work to earn money and to do what it had been planned to do. A second locomotive was delivered on 1 November 1825, built by Robert Stephenson and Company, and two more followed in 1826. The first two locomotives cost £500 each and the second two £600 each.

But the steam locomotive didn't take over immediately. And, in spite of his success with the Stockton and Darlington line, George Stephenson was still involved in the construction of other types of railway even after its opening. Bowes Railway was one of the last places to use a rope-haulage system of the type designed by

Stephenson. This line, developed to carry coal from local collieries to Jarrow on the River Tyne for shipment, originally used three rope-haulage inclines for the first 2 miles (3.2 km) and two locomotives for the final 4 miles (6.4 km). In 1826 the railway was extended to Mount Moor Colliery at Black Fell. The extension used two rope-worked inclines originally powered by a stationary steam engine at Blackham's Hill. The engine includes an 8-foot-diameter (2.4-m-diameter) drum for the east incline and a 6-foot-diameter (1.8-m-diameter) drum for the west side. Wagons were hauled up over the 'kip' (hump) to relieve the tension in the rope and enable its release from the leading wagon. Downward runs were made on the brake only with the drum out of gear. Today you can still see it all working at the Bowes Railway Centre. The only difference to the original workings is that a 300-horsepower (224 kw) electrical engine, installed in 1950, now operates the incline. You can still see steam there though, because the centre has a collection of over eighty colliery wagons and three saddle-tank steam locos. Visitors can travel on locos and traditional brake vans and see the two working inclines at Blackham's Hill. These are the only two standard-gauge rope-worked inclines in the world.

Back on the Stockton and Darlington Railway, although there was inevitably some trouble with the early locomotives, the steam engine soon proved its superiority over horse-drawn transport, particularly because of the much greater loads it could handle. As a result the company persevered with steam locomotives and, largely thanks to the railway's locomotive foreman, Timothy Hackworth, its faith in steam was eventually realized.

Hackworth had been appointed locomotive foreman on the Stockton and Darlington Railway in May 1825 at the age of thirty-eight. He started on a salary of £150 a year plus a free house and coal, and it was his responsibility to keep the engines in running order. To do this he had only very primitive facilities and just a few staff. He established workshops at the terminus of the line in Shildon and gradually built them up to such a high standard that new engines could be constructed and major repairs undertaken there.

In 1833 the Stockton and Darlington Railway Company decided that the working of the locomotives should be looked after by contractors and Hackworth, among others, agreed to take on the work. He gave up the locomotive haulage contract in 1840 to devote all his time to his own engine-building operation, making engines not only for the Stockton and Darlington Railway, but also for other British companies and railways in Russia and Nova Scotia.

Back in the 1820s though, the founding fathers of the Stockton and Darlington Railway couldn't have foreseen that within fifteen years of the opening of their line, the whole country would be feverishly building lines, or that within forty years rail transport would have become the principal means of moving passengers and goods. It was soon realized that building railways brought great benefits, and the one that really set the ball rolling was the Liverpool and Manchester Railway. A railway between these two rapidly developing northern cities had been projected at about the time that work on the Stockton and Darlington had started. Of course, George Stephenson was the man who was chosen to do it and he was involved from the outset. At first they didn't really know what sort of transportation they were going to use for the railway. There were various possibilities. Some of the directors wanted to use horses, while others favoured using stationary steam engines with long wire ropes. Not surprisingly, Stephenson preferred locomotives to both those alternatives. He was almost alone in this; however, after many long debates he persuaded the board to give the travelling engine a chance. But where were the locomotives to come from? To find out, a competition was set up with a prize of £500 for the best locomotive engine.

The competition, named the 'Rainhill Trials', was held in 1829 near Liverpool on a stretch of line about 1¾ miles (2.8 km) long. Although a considerable number of engines were constructed with a view to competing at the trials, only four were actually entered. Each locomotive had to pull three times its own weight twenty times the length of track, a distance which was the equivalent of that from Liverpool to Manchester. Then it had to fill up with coke – the engine fuel of the day – and water and make another twenty runs along the track. The average speed with a load behind the engine had to work out to not less than 10 miles an hour (16 kmph). The competition entries included Timothy Hackworth's *Sans Pareil*. But *Rocket*, a revolutionary new design, and really the forerunner of the modern locomotive, entered by George Stephenson and his son Robert, was the most successful machine there. It outperformed *Sans Pareil* and the other two competitors with a top speed of about 30 miles an hour (48 kmph). The others were a bit of a hotchpotch, very similar to locomotives that had been built before.

Stephenson had wandered way off track with his design and had a fire-tube boiler in the true locomotive sense and lots of other interesting features. He'd come up with a revolutionary new idea that increased the power and speed of the engine relative to its weight. The main innovations he brought to the locomotive were tubes, connecting rods and a blast pipe. He did away with the business of a beam engine on top of a boiler and the complicated gears and levers of every loco-motive that had been designed up to this point. In the boiler the hot gases from the burning coal went through twenty-five tubes, which were surrounded by water. The blast pipe was used to send exhaust steam up the chimney, which Stephenson knew would improve the air draught through the firebox. It's this powerful draught that creates the familiar 'chuff, chuff' of the steam locomotive.

But Stephenson's greatest innovation was the use of connecting rods. This created a sort of direct drive from the cylinders to two crank pins on the front wheels. I've seen the remains of the original engine and it has some novel bits about it. The crank pins are like two tennis balls. The brasses on the ends of the connecting rods were hollowed out like spheres inside, so when the front axle moved on the springs it wouldn't bind up and the crank pins wouldn't get hot. It was obviously a success because it achieved the record speed of about 30 miles an hour (48 kmph), which would have seemed like a rocket in 1829 – unbelievably fast. It was a major breakthrough and marked one of the key advances in railway technology. It also confirmed Stephenson as a leading engineer of his age and as a major engineering contractor for the emerging railway network.

Timothy Hackworth's *Sans Pareil*, or *Sarsparilla* as I call it, was the only really serious competition that he faced, and you could say it was the victim of bad luck. One of the cylinders burst during the trials and the boiler almost boiled dry when the water pump failed. It wasn't a

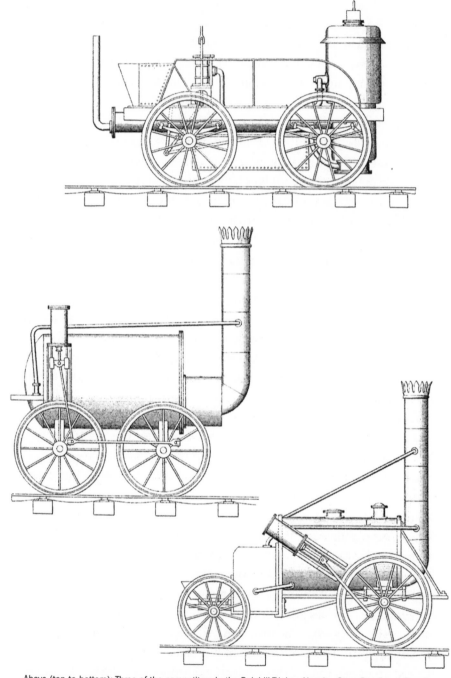

Above (top to bottom): Three of the competitors in the Rainhill Trials – *Novelty*, *Sans Pareil* and George Stephenson's famous *Rocket*.

patch on *Rocket*; the driver and fireman were at opposite ends of the locomotive, heat from the fire passed through the length of the boiler in one direction and back again, using old technology that wasn't as efficient as Stephenson's multi-tube boiler. However, the cylinders were the originals made by Stephenson and when one burst some believed that Stephenson had sabotaged his rival.

While the trials were taking place, there was a disaster along the route – the very first railway disaster on record. The locomotives were pulling carriages with passengers, and halfway along they alighted to stretch their legs. When the signal was given to reboard the train to continue the journey towards Manchester, a local MP called William Huskisson somehow managed to get in front of *Rocket* and it ran over his leg. They unhooked *Rocket*, put him on the tender and sped off to Manchester, but I'm afraid it was too late and poor Mr Huskisson died. At the side of the track there is a monument in memory of him.

Sadly, *Rocket*'s prize for winning turned out to be just a few year's service on the Liverpool and Manchester Railway before being sold to work as a freight engine. She was, after all, only a prototype and was soon replaced by more refined production models. But her basic design principles had been ground-breaking and were included in all the steam locomotive designs, that followed.

Today the original *Rocket* is in the Science Museum in London, but they've got a working replica of it at the National Railway Museum in York which runs on a track outside the museum, and another replica inside. The one inside is sliced in two so you can see all the inner workings. It's clear what a massive breakthrough in locomotive design *Rocket* was, because nearby you can see and compare it to one of the last of the old designs that preceded it, *Agenoria*, built in 1829 by Foster, Rasterick and Company. In *Agenoria* the steam pumps the pistons up and down, working vertically rather than horizontally, as later steam locomotives do. The engine is a complex system of beams and bars. It developed from the technology invented for static machinery. The rocking beams and complicated rods and levers took the power out of the piston that was meant to drive locomotive wheels. The single flue through the boiler channelled hot gases from the locomotive's fire to heat the water. It worked, but was not a very efficient means of steam production. Some collieries used huge 'kettles' beside the line to ensure the water was already hot when it was pumped into the boiler. The problem was that Foster, Rasterick and Company hadn't got to grips with how things had to change to create a mobile engine. The chimney had to be patched and repaired, because the vertical motion made the engine rock about. It dragged itself along, after a fashion, and was in operation for thirty-five years at Shutt End colliery in Staffordshire, but it was no *Rocket*!

The Liverpool and Manchester Railway was the biggest railway engineering project ever undertaken up to this point. It was not just the revolution in mechanical engineering that made it so significant; it was also a major step forward in civil engineering. When the railway was opened in 1830, it possessed two unusual engineering features: Chat Moss and Olive Mount Cuttings. Chat Moss was a great bog, which had been described as too difficult an obstacle to be crossed. George Stephenson, however, devised a floating road with hurdles interwoven with heather and constructed a water course out of empty tar barrels covered with clay. Not only did these prove to be efficient in supporting the weight of the track and trains, but this section of the line proved to be the most satisfactory. The Olive Mount Cuttings presented a different type of problem. As it was 2 miles (3.2 km) long and more than 100 feet (30.5 m) deep in places, it involved the removal of nearly half a million cubic feet (14,158 m^3)of stone. Besides Chat Moss and Olive Mount Cuttings there were several viaducts and bridges and also a tunnel. The rails were made of wrought iron, a metal that would bend without breaking, and were attached to stone blocks embedded in the ground.

After his wonderful success with the Liverpool and Manchester Railway and the winning engine, George Stephenson turned all his energies into locomotive building and the planning of other railways. Robert Stephenson ran his father's locomotive works, where the successful *Rocket* locomotive had been built under his direction. His great works, Robert Stephenson and Company at Forth Street in Newcastle upon Tyne was at the forefront of the development of the steam locomotive, and in the early years of steam it was the biggest locomotive manufacturer in the world. The works provided engines

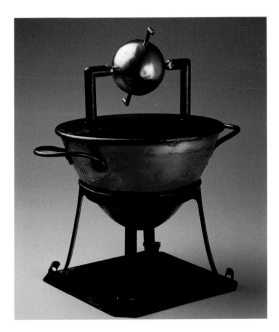

Left: A working model of Hero's aeolipile and steam boiler. The 1st century Greek mathematician found that jets of steam from the cauldron caused the hollow ball to rotate.

Below: James Watt, the Scottish engineer and inventor who is regarded as 'the father of the steam engine'.

Bottom: Watt's beam engine *circa* 1765.

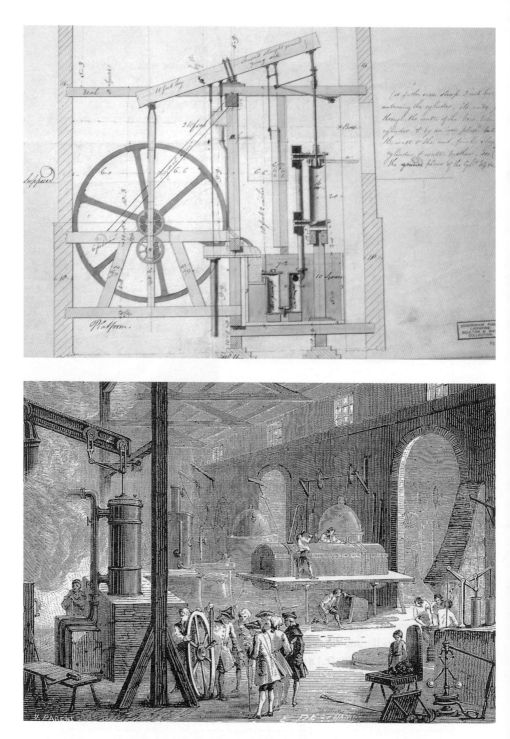

Top: Watt's original 1798 drawing for a rotative engine which he designed and built for a Manchester cotton mill. His sun and planet gear can be seen connecting the beam to the fly wheel.

Above: Boulton and Watt's Soho Engine Works, Birmingham.

Opposite: Boulton and Watt's rotative engine which was used in their works to drive machinery.

Top left: Nicholas Cugnot's steam carriage caused great alarm when it first appeared in 1769.
Top right: The Cornish engineer Richard Trevithick, who pioneered many developments in steam power but died a pauper.
Above: The world's first steam locomotive, *Pen y Darren* was built by Trevithick in 1803 to pull men and iron along a track in South Wales.

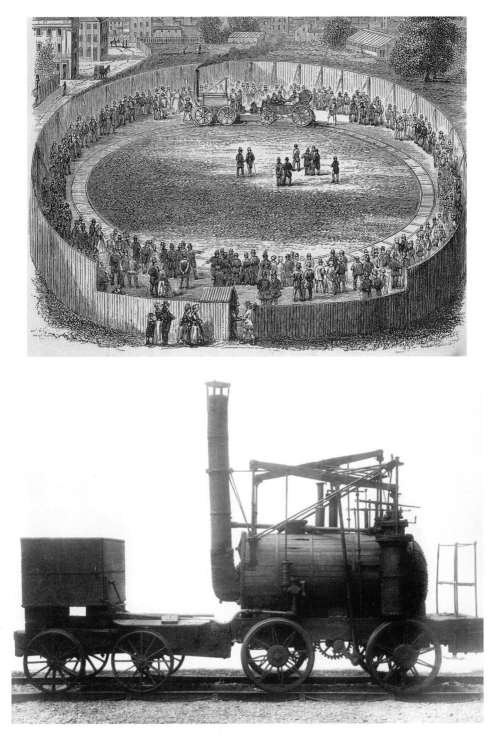

Top: Trevithick's *Catch Me Who Can* locomotive, London 1808. Passengers rode behind it on a carriage with special wheels. The novelty circular trip cost one shilling.
Above: *Puffing Billy*, designed and built by William Hedley operated from 1813 to 1873 at Wylam Colliery on Tyneside.

Right: George Stephenson, principal inventor of the steam railway locomotive.
Below: Stephenson's famous *Rocket*, winner of a Merseyside competition to find the most efficient locomotive for rail haulage. The *Rocket* ran from 1829 to 1840.

Opposite, top: Stephenson's *Locomotive* crossing Skerne bridge on the Stockton and Darlington railway. The world's first passenger railway opened in 1825.
Opposite, below: *Locomotion* was built in Robert Stephenson's Locomotive Works in Newcastle upon Tyne. They've got a fine replica at Beamish Open Air Museum which I had a ride on.

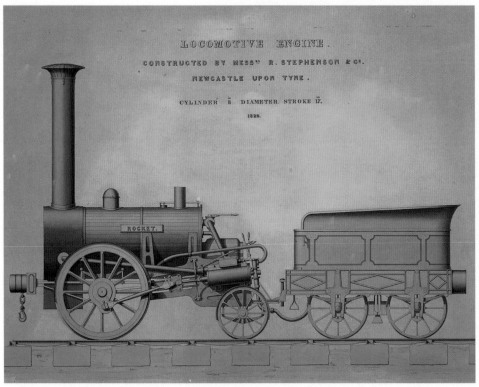

LOCOMOTIVE ENGINE.

CONSTRUCTED BY MESS" R. STEPHENSON & Cⁱ.

NEWCASTLE UPON TYNE.

CYLINDER 8 DIAMETER STROKE 17.

1829.

Top: Two freight and two passenger trains on the Liverpool and Manchester railway c.1831.
Above: The Liverpool and Manchester's great civil engineering triumph. The Chat Moss bog once considered too great an obstacle was crossed by George Stephenson's ingenious 'floating road'.

for countries all around the globe. It wasn't very long before other people jumped on the bandwagon and no doubt made locomotives for Stephenson under licence. In fact, in my home town of Bolton, Hick, Hargreaves and Company made locomotives under licence for Robert Stephenson for the American railway builders.

Meanwhile, in the development of the locomotive, Hackworth still favoured vertical cylinders on his engines. In 1831 he built six Majestic-class engines for the Stockton and Darlington Railway. Several of their design features made them very cumbersome. They rather resembled a tin of panshine, with six wheels attached and two vertical cylinders on the back. The cylinders drove a crankshaft carried below, which then drove the nearest pair of wheels. The single flue and small grate area put big limitations on the steaming power of the engine and it had an average speed of only 6 miles per hour (10 kmph).

Robert Stephenson, however, was getting closer to the true form of the locomotive. By 1830 one hundred or so locomotives had been built in Britain and most of these were of the type used in the Rainhill Trials. *Rocket* had very inclined cylinders in the beginning. Later on in its life it was noted for being top-heavy, even though it did do 30 miles an hour (48 kmph). As it was developed, the cylinders were actually lowered to be nearer to the horizontal. Stephenson then introduced the 2-2-0 *Planet* class of locomotive, which was practically identical to the modern locomotive and established the form most were to take. The main problem of the period was that they couldn't make really big castings, so they tended to produce frames for steam engines of one sort or another from two big plates of iron, sandwiched together with oak or some other hardwood in between and lots of nuts and bolts through it to give strength as well as a slight flexibility. The *Planet* class of engine had the cylinders on the inside underneath the smoke box, and the wheels and connecting rods were laid horizontally along the bottom. Another new feature was that the boiler was carried on a wooden platform outside the engine. This enabled the first *Planet*, which was a passenger engine, to be easily converted to a heavy goods locomotive by changing from 5-foot (1.5-m) driving and 3-foot (90-cm) carrying wheels to two pairs of coupled 4-foot-6-inch (1.35-m) wheels.

Progress, however, demanded more powerful locomotives and, for the comfort of the travelling public, more stability. To meet this need Robert Stephenson developed a longer framing and a longer firebox in 1841. These 'long-boilered' locomotives had all the axles in front of the firebox. They also had inside frames of iron plate and the inside cylinders shared a common steam chest between them, which had the effect of making it a better steamer. Stephenson also added another set of wheels, so the engines now had six wheels and went quite fast. The resulting locomotive, the *Patentee* 2-2-2 type, was standard for the next forty years and was used extensively in Europe. The North Eastern Railway, which had succeeded the Stockton and Darlington, had 125 long-boilers in use. The design was suitable for passenger or goods work, but the short wheelbase, dictated by the turntables in use, increasingly made it unsafe for carrying people. In spite of this, up until the 1950s there were engines still running that had been made in the 1890s and were basically of the same design. So Stephenson must have got it right when he reached that stage. You can see the sort of long-boiler locomotive that would have been built at the Forth Street works at the National Railway Museum in York. The long-boiler main-line tender engine on display there, was built to a design that had been patented by Robert Stephenson. It's fascinating to compare it with the replica of *Rocket* standing close by and it's amazing to see the massive advances that were made in locomotive design during such a short period at the beginning of Queen Victoria's reign.

In Newcastle upon Tyne the original building of Robert Stephenson and Company can still be seen. The Institute of Civil Engineers regarded Robert Stephenson as a genius and his achievements at South Street were immense. The South Street works was revolutionary for its time. Previously, engines had been constructed by common mechanics in collieries and engine workshops. Stephenson's factory was at the forefront of railway development, requiring and creating specialist mechanics and technical advances. Under his management the factory was a driving force in locomotive construction. By 1883 Robert Stephenson and Company had expanded to Forth Street, taking in Sussex Street and South Street, and from 1890 the company gradually moved its operations to more spacious premises in Darlington.

But Stephenson didn't just build the locomotives; he built the lines with all the stations, bridges and engineering that were involved. Newcastle's High Level Bridge, designed by Robert Stephenson and opened by Queen Victoria in 1849, was the first railway bridge across the River Tyne. The five sandstone piers and ribbed iron arches carry the railway on an upper deck and a road on the lower deck. Stephenson wouldn't let anything stand in his way. In the 1840s he was building the railway from London to Holyhead. When he reached Conwy he not only had a river to cross, which he did with his tubular bridge, but he also had to bypass a castle and get under the medieval town walls. The basic design of his bridge involved two rectangular tubes consisting of wrought-iron rolled plates which were hand-riveted together. These carried each of the tracks between the masonry abutments. The tubes, which weighed 1,300 tons each, were pre-fabricated on the shore and floated under the abutments by means of pontoons. They were then raised into position by hydraulic presses. The whole thing must have been a heck of a job, and at one point Stephenson said: 'The difficulty we are contending with is much greater than I anticipated, but I will never give up.'

Because George and Robert Stephenson were involved in much of the early development of the railways, most railways adopted their 4-foot-8½-inch (1.41-m) gauge. As this became established, other engineers followed suit. The one big exception was Isambard Kingdom Brunel and the Great Western Railway. Most of the early development of the railways had been done in the north of England. But down in the south they were catching up, and it was the merchants of Bristol who took the lead here. They decided that they wanted a railway that would run from Bristol all the way to London, and in 1833 the Bristol Chamber of Commerce sanctioned the building of a quadruple line of railway between the two cities. The man who got the job of creating this for them was the famous and celebrated engineer Brunel, who was twenty-seven years old when he received the commission.

Six months after Brunel's appointment the name Great Western Railway was adopted and has remained ever since. The route was to run via Reading and Bath, a course selected because of easier gradients and possible extensions to be added. So, while Robert Stephenson was building the London and Birmingham Railway and the line to Holyhead, Brunel was constructing his Great Western Railway. Brunel was a man who had very wide interests, but what made him the most outstanding and influential of all the great engineers of the nineteenth century was his ability to succeed at anything he turned his hand to. Brunel's projects were astonishing for their scale, their versatility and their daring. His Great Western Railway was a magnificent feat of engineering. He surveyed most of it himself from the back of a horse and stopped in some pretty ropy inns and digs on his way. The bridges, viaducts and tunnels that he made were quite fantastic. He even designed the lamp-posts for the stations, acted in the capacity of a director of the station hotel at Paddington, and, when the going got tough, he was not above getting down to doing some actual digging on the line itself.

Brunel's vision was one of a complete railway system, which would include innovations in architecture, track work, motive power and, importantly, track gauge. But the man was a bit of a wayward genius. When he designed his railway, he felt that the lines being built by the Stephensons were too narrow, so he decided to make his wider. Instead of adopting George and Robert Stephenson's 4-foot-8½-inch (1.41-m) gauge, Brunel decided that his railway would be 7 foot ¼ inch (2.1 m) wide in between the rails. This, he felt, would enable the building of more powerful locomotives and wide carriages. He also urged the use of timber to support the rails instead of stone blocks. Although it used more land, track laid at this broad gauge and the trains designed to run on it gave a faster, smoother, and more fuel-efficient ride. If that width had been kept, the size of trains today and the speeds that they would have been able to achieve would really have been something.

When Brunel was asked about it later, he couldn't remember when it was that he had decided to opt for the wide gauge. He said, 'I think the impression grew on me gradually.' He didn't seem to see it as a problem that all the rest of the railways in the country were being built to a different gauge. He thought his wide gauge would mean faster and more comfortable trains on his Great Western Railway. At the time he couldn't see that there would be many people travelling the length of the country by train, and for those who did, he didn't think it would be a problem to change trains when they went from the lines of one railway company on to his.

The building of the Great Western line involved many difficulties, and valleys and rivers had to be crossed. But by 1838 it was open from London to Taplow, where the railway crossed the River Thames over the longest and flattest brick arches ever built – a record that still stands today. This bridge, with two main spans of 128 feet (39 m) of semi-elliptical form and a rise of only 24 feet (7 m), was a remarkable structure. The Brent valley was spanned by a viaduct 960 feet (293 m) long. The terminus in London was originally going to be Euston, shared with the London and Birmingham Railway. Construction soon started, however, on the Great Western's own terminal in the suburb of Paddington. The first section of the line from Paddington to Taplow was opened in 1838, then extended to Twyford and then Reading. From London to Chippenham the line was so flat that they called it 'Brunel's billiard table', but between Chippenham and Bath he had to get through the massive barrier of the 400-foot-high (122-m) Box Hill. It involved a lot of deep cutting and a tunnel, which, at nearly 2 miles (3.2 km) in length, was by far the greatest railway tunnel that had ever been attempted. It was an immense undertaking and, apart from the steam pumps, which kept the workings clear of water, and the gunpowder, which was used to blast the rock, it was all accomplished by the strength of men and horses working by candlelight. Many people had said that the construction of this tunnel would be impossible, but Brunel drove it through. It cost £100 per yard to build and for two-and-a-half years its construction consumed a ton of gunpowder a week. The tunnel was completely straight and, in a final touch of virtuosity, it was designed so that the sun shone through it from end to end at dawn on Brunel's birthday on 9 April.

By June 1841, the whole line was open and Brunel began to plan numerous branches to towns and cities near its route, such as Oxford and Cheltenham, as well as an extension to Exeter, which would span the River Tamar at Saltash. Brunel's Royal Albert Suspension Bridge was built at Saltash between 1854 and 1857. The soundness of his engineering means that even today, although the broad gauge has long disappeared, trains speed over a virtually unchanged railway at 125 miles per hour (201 kmph).

There is an intriguing story about Brunel's broad-gauge railway. When the railway was first planned, it was his intention to have locomotives for his new line built by manufacturers to specifications he had produced himself. But if Brunel had what he called a weak point, it was the fact that he wasn't good at designing locomotives. Although he was a brilliant civil engineer, his efforts at locomotive design were not quite as successful. In fact, his early attempts became known as 'freaks' and it was reported that they could hardly pull themselves along, let alone a train, so they were quietly forgotten about. If you look at his drawings and at one example that was actually manufactured, it's clear that they weren't very good, which is a bit unusual for Brunel because he had a wonderful eye for beautiful things. So, to look after the locomotive-building side of the business, he enlisted the services of a man called Daniel Gooch as his locomotive superintendent.

Gooch's first job was to get hold of some locomotives for the line as quickly as possible, because they'd got a railway line with no engines to run on it. Gooch was only twenty-one, but he had already worked with Robert Stephenson at his Forth Street locomotive works and through this connection he was able to secure the purchase of two engines from the company, which had been originally intended for a 5-foot-6-inch (1.7-m) gauge railway in the United States. The scheme had failed and Gooch adapted them for the 7-foot (2.1-m) gauge. Named *North Star* and *Morning Star* they were the first locomotives to run on the Great Western in 1837.

It was not until Daniel Gooch designed the *Firefly* fleet that the Great Western had a locomotive fleet of its own that it could rely on. Unfortunately, none of his broad-gauge locos survived when the Great Western's wide gauge was scrapped in the 1890s, and to get an idea of what they were like we have to rely on the activities of a dedicated bunch of enthusiasts who are having a go at building a replica. At Didcot Railway Centre in Oxfordshire a group of volunteers who call themselves the Firefly Trust are currently in the process of constructing a replica broad-gauge *Firefly* locomotive.

As the Great Western Railway expanded its network in other directions, Brunel took charge of each line, always laying broad gauge. The South Devon line presented particular problems because it had to be built between the sea and the cliffs at Dawlish. This made it necessary to build a sea wall to protect the railway. The line extended into Cornwall, with many timber viaducts built over deep valleys. Pleasing as they were to the eye, they were later replaced by more durable structures. The railway was also stretching into the Midlands, an area firmly held by the narrower-gauge systems. Lines were absorbed from Swindon to Gloucester and Cheltenham, Oxford to Didcot, and Reading to Hungerford and Basingstoke. This incursion into narrow-gauge country caused such controversy that it became known as the 'Battle of the Gauges'.

Brunel never really stopped his inquisitive mind trying to find other ways for locomotion besides the steam engine. One of his ill-fated ventures was the 'atmospheric' railway. This consisted of a cast-iron pipe laid between the rails with a continuous slot on the upper side and an arm connecting an internal piston with the vehicles moving over it. When the air was exhausted from the pipe, the piston was driven forward by atmospheric pressure, taking the train with it. If the materials had been a little better and the rats hadn't eaten the zip fastener that went along the top of the tube, it could possibly have been a success and the development of the railways would have been very different. As it was, Brunel expended a lot of money, time energy and thought into this 'atmospheric' railway and in the end it all came to nothing.

Around the country locomotive design was improving rapidly in the quest for greater speed and stability. One of the designs of this time was developed by Thomas Russell Crampton, an engineer working under Daniel Gooch in Swindon. He took out a patent in 1842 for an express locomotive with a large boiler and driving wheels but with a low centre of gravity. In his design the driving axle was placed right at the base of the frame behind the firebox. To keep the connecting rods as short as possible the cylinders were displaced rearwards outside the frames and fed from the smokebox by prominent outside steam pipes. The motion and valve gear was all placed outside, allowing the boiler to be sunk down in the frames, which had the effect of making the engine very wide. Crampton's engines were very popular on the continent. During trials for these engines on the Grand Junction Railway they were taken up by the London and North-Western Railway, which built one for itself in 1847. Crampton's locomotives could reach speeds of 90 miles per hour (145 kmph), but were not popular in Britain because of the uncomfortable ride and the destructive effect they had on the track, a direct result of the low driving axle. A British engine built to this design by J. E. Connell of the London and North Western Railway had the nickname 'Mac's Mangle' because of the destruction it caused.

Throughout the 1830s and 1840s people all over Britain were clamouring for new lines and money was being thrown at these developments to such an extent that the phenomenon was given the name of 'railway mania'. Within twenty years of the Rainhill Trials around 5,000 miles (8,047 km) of track criss-crossed the country. The nineteenth-century railway pioneers brought the British nation to the forefront of the world stage in the realm of civil engineering. The construction of the lines involved such feats of engineering that it seems incredible that these were accomplished in the days when precision tools and mechanical aids to labour were unknown. Railway contractors working for engineers like Brunel and the Stephensons employed thousands of construction workers to dig and blast their way through soil and rock, changing the whole landscape with cuttings and tunnels, bridges, embankments and viaducts. It was the men who had built the canals, the navigators or 'navvies', as they were called, who were put to good use on the railways within a very short period after the completion of most of the English canal system. They would all have been out of work if it hadn't been for the railways. It is said that the navvies tunnelling underneath the Pennine chain, where there was a constant threat of roof falls, lived on steak and gin and were drunk most of the time. It was astounding how many yards of earth a man could move with a wheelbarrow and a shovel.

It must have been an unbelievably exciting time. Unlike motorways that can follow the rise and fall of the land, canals had to have level ground, except when there was an obstacle that could not be got round. Then locks or, occasionally tunnels had to be built. The railways also needed ground as flat as possible and some unbelievable cuttings and embankments were constructed to achieve this. The tunnelling was exceptional. A lot of people died in the creation of the railways and it took many years, but the navvies completed the work nevertheless. The question of health and safety didn't really arise. This is reflected in a contemporary report of an accident that occured when Brunel was building the bridge at Saltash. They were lifting great iron girders when something went wrong with a winch. It ripped one of the operatives in half and a great block of stone came down, which hit the plinth round the bottom of one of the pillars. The report stated that even though the man died, which was bad news, the base of the pillar wasn't damaged! It didn't knock the moulding off the bottom – incredible! Another story was about a chap who got his arm blown off when they were blasting their way through a tunnel. They didn't sack him or throw him out, but found him a soft job. He ended up driving a winding engine at the top of one of the airshafts which were used for winding up the earth they cleared as they were driving the tunnel down below.

As the railway network spread, locomotive design made very rapid advances and the engines became more streamlined and pleasing to the eye. One chap called Patrick Stirling made some beautiful, graceful engines. Stirling was locomotive superintendent at the Glasgow and South-Western Railway from 1853 and later the chief locomotive superintendent of the Great Northern Railway. He had a saying that a locomotive with connecting rods holding three, four or six wheels together was like a lad running with his pants down. His earlier engines with domed boilers and no cab led up to his greatest achievement: the 8-foot (2.4-m) 4-2-2 singles constructed from 1870 onwards at Doncaster. They were almost like great mill engines with 7- or 8-foot (2.1- or 2.4-m) driving wheels and two huge connecting rods to the ends of the piston rods. They had no humps on the top of the boiler, just the funnel at the front and the cab at the back – though it was hardly a cab, being only about 18 inches (45.7 cm) deep. The engines went at 60 miles an hour (97 kmph), so if you were up there on the footplate with the wind and rain blowing away it must have been bad news, especially going backwards. But going forwards in decent weather it was magic. Stirling built a lot of these locos and they were used by all main-line trains for the next twenty-five years. In the 1890s there was an annual Race to the North and in 1895 trains pulled by these Patrick Stirling locomotives achieved average speeds of 80 miles per hour (129 kmph) between London and York. There is one still in existence in York's National Railway Museum.

Near the end of the nineteenth century Francis Webb, who was chief mechanical engineer of the London and North-Western Railway, perfected the compounding of locomotive cylinders. This actually means that the steam is used twice. I don't know whether it gave them any more power, but it certainly made them more economical. Instead of the steam going through the cylinders and straight up the chimney as it did in everybody else's locomotives, Webb's *LNWR No. 66* calmed the process of expansion down a bit. His engine had two outside cylinders using high-pressure steam straight from the boiler, which does its business shoving the piston driving the rear axle. Then it goes through a chamber and is used again in the low-pressure cylinder, which was inside driving the leading axle. By this point the steam has practically expended nearly all its energy and it goes out up the chimney. It definitely made a great difference in the amount of coal burned. The driving axles were not coupled and this sometimes resulted in one pair of wheels revolving in a different direction from the other wheels when starting the engine! The best examples were the *Teutonic* class of 1889 with their large boilers and 7-foot-1-inch (2.1-m) driving wheels, which achieved a start-to-stop speed of 64 miles per hour (103 kmph) from London to Crewe.

In the 1880s and 1890s there were a lot of major developments in locomotive design. Every different railway company had its own great works and the famous railway towns came into being: Crewe was the centre for the London and North-Western Railway; Doncaster for the Great Northern Railway; Derby for the Midland Railway; and Swindon for the Great Western Railway. Near Bolton, at a place called Horwich, the Lancashire and Yorkshire Railway started off on a green-field site in the 1800s. A great locomotive works was constructed where literally thousands of locomotives were made over a period up to around 1960.

On the Great Western, the high point of the broad-gauge era was the *Iron Duke* 4-2-2 express locomotives, which were built at Gooch's Swindon works from 1851 onwards. These powerful engines were the mainstay of the company's express passenger services. But although the broad gauge created a great stir, with people flocking to see it and reported speeds of 90 miles per hour (145 kmph), it certainly had its critics. Travel between the Great Western and other railways made it necessary for goods and passengers to change trains when going out of the Great Western area. Standardization was called for, and so in 1845 the Gauge Committee sat to decide on the matter. They organized some high-speed trial runs. Daniel Gooch's 7-foot (2.1-m) gauge *Ixion* achieved 60 miles per hour (97 kmph) pulling an 80-ton train against a Stephenson 4-2-0 standard gauge, which reached 53 miles per hour (85 kmph). Despite the broad gauge being considered far superior, it was the standard gauge that was selected, almost entirely because of the fact that by this time there was far more of the narrower-gauge track in existence. An Act of Parliament in 1848 enforced this, so the Great Western had to lay a third line throughout its system. Brunel's broad gauge lasted until 1892, when it was abolished completely. Sadly, nothing remains whatsoever of the 7-foot (2.1-m) gauge. The only thing we've got now to remind us of it all is the *Firefly* replica they're building at Didcot.

In spite of losing the 'Battle of the Gauges', the Great Western Railway grew and grew. George Jackson Churchward became locomotive superintendent in 1902 and produced designs for a range of Great Western locomotives that were well ahead of their time. His aim was to create a set of standardized locomotive designs for express passenger work, heavy freight, mixed traffic and tank engines. The work that had been begun by Churchward was continued and expanded upon by C. B. Collett, who took over from him in 1922. His *Castle* and *King* designs became something of a benchmark for express passenger development. When the railways were regrouped in 1923, the Great Western was the only company out of the newly created 'Big Four' (the Great Western; the Southern; the London, Midland and Scottish; and the London and North-Eastern Railways) to retain its original name. It now became one of the largest and most successful railway companies in the world. By the 1930s the Great Western and its gleaming Brunswick-green steam locos had become familiar names in homes throughout the nation. Today you can still catch a glimpse of the golden age of steam locomotion on the Great Western at the Didcot Railway Centre, where they have a magnificent collection of Great Western locomotives in steam, as well as a stretch of broad-gauge track and the *Firefly* replica.

CHAPTER THREE

DRIVING THE WHEELS
OF INDUSTRY

Steam power had first developed out of the need to pump water from mines as they got deeper, and for the production of materials in quantities that were too great for the limited strength of animal and human power. Between 1790 and 1800, the decade when Trevithick made his great breakthrough with high-pressure steam, more steam engines of every kind were built than in the rest of the eighteenth century put together. This great expansion in engine building, along with the experiments in applying steam power to locomotion begun by Trevithick and carried on by men like George Stephenson, were indications of a number of changes that became known as the Industrial Revolution. These trends included things like the substitution of machines for human effort. Then there was the substitution of mechanical sources of power for natural sources like water and, finally, the exploitation and transportation of raw materials and manufactured products.

Many of these changes, which were to have such a massive impact, first on Britain and then on the rest of the world, were happening at the same time. So, as Richard Trevithick was developing the first steam railways, he was also involved in pioneering work in other branches of steam power. In 1805 he adapted his high-pressure engine to drive an iron rolling mill and propel a barge with the aid of paddle wheels. His engine also powered the world's first steam dredgers and drove a threshing machine on a farm. However, in spite of the fact that he was an extremely important early pioneer, Trevithick's lack of business thinking would prove to be his downfall. In 1811 he was declared bankrupt after a partner used one of his ideas to establish his own operation. Undeterred by this setback, Trevithick carried on developing

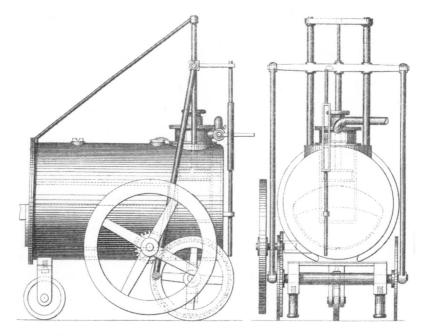

Above: Trevithick's *Kensington* locomotive circa 1800.

new ideas. In 1812 he completed the first 'portable' steam engine, mounted on wheels. This could be pulled by a horse to wherever it was needed, so it could have been a boon to agriculture. But farming was an unstable industry at the time and many farmers were reluctant to spend money on something they were not sure about. It was another twenty years before the portable engine was taken up by farming the community.

In 1815, nine of Trevithick's engines were ordered for the Peruvian silver mines and, dreaming of unlimited mineral wealth in the Andes, he sailed to South America in 1816. When he returned in 1827, after making and losing a fortune all over South America, he found that steam transport had become a thriving concern and other engineers, notably George Stephenson, had profited from his inventions. Trevithick, by contrast, had been overtaken by events. When he died in 1833, he was living in Dartford, Kent, where he was being employed on some of his inventions by John Hall. He was lodging at the time at the Bull Inn, but he had outlived his earnings and was in debt to the innkeeper. He would have been buried at the expense of the parish, but his friends at the factory raised enough cash to give the 'great inventor' a decent burial in Dartford churchyard, where he lies without a stone to mark his resting place.

Richard Trevithick was one of the greatest figures in the history of steam, but he died homeless and penniless. His achievements, though, brought wealth to many other people and his innovations were copied extensively. In 1803 for example, his former teacher, William Murdock, who was by this time running Boulton and Watt, began experimenting with high-pressure steam for the company's engines and it wasn't long before Boulton and Watt engines were adapted to high pressure.

The period from 1800 to 1870 was a time of unparalleled prosperity for Cornwall, thanks, in no small part, to the advances that Trevithick made in steam power, for pumping water from the tin mines and for winding ore from them. The development of the beam engine carried on for years and years, long after James Watt and Trevithick. In Cornwall there were one or two noted iron founders like Harvey of Hayle, which made very modern examples, who kept on making beam engines right up to the 1900s. And then there was Holman Bros, which made compressors for rock drills for use in the tin mines. From mining followed other industrial activities, at first associated with mining and the machinery required for deep hard-rock mining. Important iron foundries were established to build steam engines for mine pumping, and this expertise led to the 'Cornish engine' being adapted for all manner of purposes, including pumping London's sewage and dewatering Holland's polders. The success of the Cornish engine meant that it was quickly put into use all over the world.

The steam engine became an integral part of Cornish mining for two-and-a-half centuries. The first Cornish miners concentrated on washing tin ore out of deposits near the surface. However, the coming of the steam engine enabled the miners to pump water from these increasingly deeper mines, raise ore to the surface and then crush it. At the height of the mining industry in the 1860s there were over 650 beam engines working in Cornwall. Today the picture that most people have of Cornwall is one of holiday beaches and picturesque fishing villages, but in the eighteenth and nineteenth centuries the county was a key industrial area as a result of its massive deposits of tin and copper ore. In those days I don't think you would've gone to Cornwall for a holiday. For one thing it was very hard to get there by means of horse and carriage. But if you imagine the amount of tin-mine chimneys that were all belching out smoke, it would probably have looked a bit like Lancashire did a hundred years later.

There are one or two survivors of the original tin-mine beam engine left down in Cornwall and perhaps the most dramatic is the Levant Beam Engine, which is situated on a cliff top just 5 miles (8 km) from Land's End. This great mine was opened in 1820 and its original engine still survives. At its peak of production the mine extended for a mile underneath the Atlantic Ocean. It was one of the most successful in the area, mining both tin and copper ores. In 1919 a terrible disaster occurred there. The engine driver who was working the machinery complained to the management that it was making funny noises. He thought it wasn't too healthy and said that if they didn't do something about it he was going to resign and move on to another mine. But the management didn't do anything about it, so he resigned and went to another mine. A fortnight later the pump rod came off the end of the beam and the whole lot went down the shaft with about thirty men who were all doomed – very sad. Obviously there were no health and safety inspectors then and the management were only interested in making money, so they took no notice of the driver's warning.

Cornwall had led the way in the development of steam power, and by the end of the eighteenth century steam engines were in operation in many of the county's tin and copper mines. But steam power wasn't quite as widespread in other parts of the country and by the year 1800 the steam engine had still not made such a transformation in industry as is often imagined. Water power continued very much in evidence, but the new industries – cotton manufacture, iron smelting, mining and engineering – were gradually changing over to the new source of power: steam. As time went by, they needed to fire up their steam engines and so they had to go where the coal was – hence the growth of great industrial areas in the coal fields of the Midlands, the North-east, South Wales, Lancashire and Yorkshire. In places like Wigan coal was sticking out of the ground 5 feet (1.5 m) thick and they could easily get it to feed the greedy steam engines. Great chimneys were built with clouds of black smoke belching out. It must've been much nicer to live in the country. Certainly the factory owners always used to build a beautiful house upwind from their works.

The development of the steam engine by Newcomen, Watt and Trevithick not only pumped water out of mines and enabled mining to take place much deeper than before, but also revolutionized the lives of the mine workers. Some of the hardest work was done by the women who worked in the Scottish coal-mining industry in the eighteenth century. They were the bearers whose job it was to haul huge amounts of coal from the coalface to the shaft. Some even had to carry it up ladders to the surface. Robert Bald went to find out about this and published a report of his findings in 1812. He found one woman's load to be as heavy as 170 lbs (77 kg). She had to carry this 150 yards (137 m) to the mine shaft, climb 117 feet (35.7 m) of ladders to the surface and then haul it a further 20 yards (18.2 m) to the store. This would be repeated up to twenty-four times in one shift and amounted to carrying 2 tons of coal a day on her back. The steam engine changed all this. Not only did it pump, but it could also be used to turn a wheel and winding gear to haul workers, and materials up and down the shafts.

The large coal deposits in Britain were one of the most important contributing factors to the development of steam and the Industrial Revolution. It was the unlocking of Britain's coal seams that turned the country into a great manufacturing state. The steam engine provided the power to drain the coal mines, which supplied the fuel that was needed for newly developed methods of smelting iron, which then, in turn, provided the metal used in the construction of engines and machines. At the start of the nineteenth century, as the Age of Steam began to reach its peak, Britain was on the verge of becoming the greatest industrial nation in the world and the engineers who helped to achieve this became the heroes of the day.

Steam power by itself did not cause the Industrial Revolution, but it was an important contributing factor. The factory system had developed originally out of the textile industry and this was before and quite separate from the application of steam power to industry in general. The role of water power is nearly always underestimated, probably because the steam engine has always provided a dramatic image of what we think of as industrialization. But as late as the 1820s more cotton was manufactured using water power than steam power, and the use of steam for locomotion was still in its very early stages. In many cases water power and steam power were employed side by side. A good example of this can be seen at Coldharbour Mill at Uffculme near Cullompton in Devon. The mill started its working life nearly 200 years ago spinning wool and worsted yarn, and the biggest change it saw in that time was the arrival of steam power. But that wasn't until 1865. Until then it had been run entirely by water power, and even after the steam engine had been installed, the waterwheel continued to be used and it provided power for the night shift right up to 1978.

Another good place to see how steam and water power were used together is in Quarry Bank Mill at Styal, just round the back of Manchester Airport. When the mill was built in the second half of the eighteenth century, water provided the power for all the revolutionary new spinning machines. As it was enlarged in the nineteenth century it needed more power, so steam engines, which were first introduced from 1810 onwards, were brought in to supplement the water power, especially during the drier months of the summer.

In the early part of the nineteenth century, as more firms began to manufacture steam engines, the capacity of industry to generate steam power began to grow slowly but surely. The biggest change that this brought about was that mill and factory owners could now break away from the need to build their premises near flowing water. Coldharbour Mill and Quarry Bank Mill are both situated by the side of rivers in rural settings. But the steam engine meant that industry could now move location to the new and expanding towns. Even so, it was not until the mid 1830s that the use of steam exceeded that of water power. After this the spread of the steam engine was rapid, and by the middle of the century steam had become the primary source of power, not just in textiles but also in other factory industries and most heavy industries including iron and steel manufacturing.

The earliest factories had been built for only ten or twenty people to work in, but by the middle of the nineteenth century a single factory might employ hundreds of workers and operate many different types of machinery. As the steam engine took over the role of the waterwheel, the power from a single engine or a series of engines was used to power dozens and dozens of machines in places like textile mills and engineering works. Power was transmitted by hundreds of yards of line shafts and belts. The power of the steam engine passed through horizontal shafts and toothed gearing to vertical shafts. Through yet more toothed gearing, these drove horizontal shafts on each floor of the factory or works connected to individual machines by leather belts and pulleys. Horizontal line shafts were usually between 6½ feet (2 m) and 16½ feet (5 m) in length. They were coupled together using bearings and hangers or brackets to enable them to run the whole length of a mill or factory floor – which could be as long as 200 feet (61 m).

This can all be seen at Queen Street Mill in Burnley. Here you can still observe how the single-storey weaving shed was powered by a tandem compound steam engine constructed by the firm of Robert of Nelson. Today the weaving shed houses around 300 machines, but originally there were over 1,000 looms and machines clanging away, all powered by a system of shafts and belts driven by the steam engine. Saltaire Mill, built in 1853 by the River Aire in Yorkshire, was six storeys high and 548 feet (167 m) long. It was said to accommodate over 1,200 looms in its massive weaving shed. The 9,843 feet (3,000 m) of shafting weighed over 60 tons and needed four beam engines with an output of 1,250 horsepower (932.5 kw) to operate the machinery. This system of steam engines, toothed gearing, line shafting and leather belts continued as the chief method of transmitting power in British factories throughout the nineteenth century. In fact, there was still a car manufacturer near London which used line shafting right up to the 1930s.

There was also the rope-drive system, which was used at Ellen Road Mill near Rochdale, and at Trencherfield Mill at Wigan pier which houses one of the world's last working mill steam engines with its enormous 26-foot (8-m) flywheel. Ropes were connected to grooved pulleys on the flywheel of a steam engine and transmitted the power to shafting on each floor. This method was first introduced to factories in Belfast during the 1850s. Very quickly it became the principal power system in Lancashire cotton mills. Rope-drive was used in other industries too, from brick works to iron-rolling mills.

This rapid expansion in the use of the steam engine meant that more and more coal was needed. It was required in factories and in iron works and for providing the fuel for the many new kinds of steam engines. With the invention of steam locomotives and steam ships, this demand reached new heights. Between 1770 and 1860 the amount of coal mined in Britain grew from 6 million to 66 million tons.

Whenever we think of steam power, we tend to think of the great cotton and woollen mills in Lancashire and Yorkshire or about engines that did the pumping and drove the pithead winding gear in mines. But throughout the nineteenth century steam power was applied to a wide variety of other industries. One very important use was in saw-mills. Until this time a great baulk of wood or a huge tree either had to be adzed into the square or hung over a pit with a man down the hole and a man up top operating a saw by hand, about 8 feet (2.4 m) long. It must have taken forever to cut a slab off the side of a great tree trunk, but the steam engine changed all that. There was a sawmill in Bolton I remember, with a big cast-iron beam over the main entrance bearing the words 'Steam Sawmill'. So some were still being run on steam power until quite recently.

Another of the new applications for steam power was printing. As early as 1814 Frederick Koening, a Saxon printer living in London, had invented a press in which the type bed was propelled backwards and forwards by steam power. The paper was fed around a cylinder, which pressed down on top of the type bed. The invention was taken up immediately by John Walter, the owner of *The Times*. Until this time the only source of power available to the printer had been that of his own muscles, and however strong he was and however great his efforts, the number of impressions of which he was capable was limited to around 200 an hour at the most. The new machine could print 1,000 impressions an hour. Walter claimed that this was 'the greatest improvement connected with printing since the discovery of the art itself'.

Above: A steam-powered printing press in the 1840s. In all areas of industry, steam power meant faster turnover and increased production.

Industrialization brought about major changes in the way goods were made and it transformed the ways in which people lived. Agricultural workers fled from rural poverty to become factory hands, swapping village life for town life. The landscape began to change dramatically as steam drove the Industrial Revolution forward. Towns were full of machinery, great tall chimneys billowing smoke, buildings that rattled and trembled all day where the piston of the steam engine worked monotonously up and down. Between 1801 and 1851 Britain's population nearly doubled. More than half of these people lived in towns and worked in the mills, mines and factories.

But these industrial towns could only be supported by an agricultural system that generated enough food. So the introduction of the steam engine into agriculture was crucial. Early on all agricultural machinery was driven by horse gins and the like, or muscle power with a contraption like bevel gears and a long wooden arm with a horse anchored to the end of it. Of course the poor horse went round in a circle all day with its bag of oats hanging on its neck and worked the gears that actually turned the wheel to work threshing machines.

The first farm in the world to use steam power was in north Wales in 1798, and a year later a steam engine was used to thresh corn in East Lothian. It's no surprise that the East Lothian farm was located next door to a coal mine where steam engines were already in use. But it took another half-century before steam power came into common use in agriculture when small 'portable' engines were developed to replace stationary ones. Eventually, by the 1840s, they'd developed a small steam engine that could be pulled by a horse to the farmyard and attached to a threshing box to thresh the corn. This was a wonderful advance, which was followed a little later by the steam plough, which could do the work previously done by a team of horses.

The use of steam power in the nineteenth century was a much more varied business than it had been in the eighteenth. Apart from the revolution in transport brought about by the railways and the development of the iron-hulled steamship, steam engines of many different kinds were being applied in large numbers to all sorts of jobs. But until the middle of the nineteenth century the basic design was still the beam engine that had been developed by James Watt. And despite the success of the Stockton and Darlington and the Liverpool and Manchester Railways there were still supporters of the idea of using stationary engines to provide the motive power for railways until the 1830s at least. After all, it was an idea that was already very well established. The world's first engines were all stationary, built beside mine shafts to pump water away. They were then used to pull wagons up hills from the mines by hauling a rope and were even used on main-line railways when locomotive power was not enough. The Liverpool and Manchester itself could easily have been rope-hauled if some of the directors had been able to get the system they wanted.

There is a large stationary engine at the National Railway Museum in York that gives us an idea of what things could have been like. It was built in 1833 for the Stanhope and Tyne Railway to exploit limestone deposits. Stationary engines like this, using a rope-haulage system, were cheap to use in hilly areas and were operating railways at most early mineral quarries. This engine was able to haul six wagons at a time up a track a mile long. It drove a winding drum carrying a long rope, which would drag wagons of limestone up the steep Weatherill incline near Stanhope in County Durham. The limestone was taken on by railway to blast furnaces at Consett and elsewhere.

The steam used in this engine was heated in a boiler and entered the engine through a cylinder, which pushed the piston, giving the wheel a half-turn and, as the valve moved, a second channel opened, allowing steam in to move the piston back again. This was called a reciprocating engine and it was a more advanced engine than those designed by Newcomen. It was a double-acting engine because the valve allowed high-pressure steam to act alternately on both faces of the piston, whereas Newcomen's engines allowed steam in on only one side, but relied on atmospheric pressure to push the piston back into the cylinder where a vacuum had been created by the condensation of steam.

Until well into the nineteenth century the steam engine had basically been a beam engine and its different applications, like the early locomotive, involved a boiler with a beam engine on top of it. Even early ship engines were almost like beam engines. But by the 1840s and 1850s it was developing into something that was more like a flat bed with a piston, connecting rod and crankshaft, which provided direct drive to the machinery. In a rolling mill, for example, the engine would be an ordinary single-cylinder engine with reversing gear on it and the main engine spindle or the crankshaft would be connected directly to the rollers. Engines like this were a lot more compact and more strongly built.

The potential and usefulness of steam began to grow enormously as greater understanding of the scientific principles, along with the introduction of precision machine tools, brought about advances in engine design and construction. It wasn't very long ago that I repaired a steam engine that was built in 1854 by a man called Mr Dewinton in Caernarfon. All the parts of this machine were individually black-smithed. Each nut fitted on each bolt and it was stamped up so you got the right nut for the right bolt. The development of machine tools did away with all that. In Manchester Joseph Whitworth introduced precision tools that were capable of working to one hundred thousandth of an inch.

By the middle of the nineteenth century the rotative beam engine of Boulton and Watt began to give way to more modern horizontal engines. The idea of laying a cylinder on its side and coupling the piston rod to a crank without a beam in between them was actually Trevithick's, but it wasn't until later, in the 1840s, that engineers led by Matthew Murray of Leeds started to produce horizontal engines in any numbers. The simple horizontal engine was much cheaper to build, house and install than the beam engine and it transformed the steam engine into a versatile source of power that could be tailored to any kind of industry and any kind of machinery.

One of the best places to go to see a beam engine and the more advanced horizontal engine side by side and working, is at what's left of a mill called Ellenroad, which is off the M62 near Milnrow, just outside Rochdale. There we've got a grand example of a great big tandem compound engine of the horizontal type and a beam engine as well which dates from the 1860s. Both of them are in working condition. On the firing floor on steam days, coal is shovelled by hand into the mechanical stokers that feed the twin roaring furnaces of the Lancashire boiler that generate the steam.

All that remains of the original Ellenroad cotton ring-spinning mill is the engine house and the boiler house. The twins of the twin-tandem compound mill engine in the engine house are called *Victoria* and *Alexandria*. Originally built in 1892 as a triple-expansion engine, the present engines, which were rebuilt in 1921, are the result of some refurbishment that occurred after a fire destroyed the first cotton mill in 1916. A new ring-spinning mill was constructed in 1921 and the changeover from mule spinning needed more power. The engines were stopped in 1975 when electrification of the mill was completed.

The twin-tandem compound engine is so called because there are two engines, hence the 'twin'; 'tandem' because each engine has two cylinders joined by a single piston rod; and 'compound' because steam is used twice – once in the high-pressure cylinder and again in the low-pressure cylinder. In Lancashire and Yorkshire there are quite a few surviving examples of these engines. There was one at the bottom of nearly every street – a big mill engine driving a great mill about five storeys high and 200 feet square (18.6 m²). Many of the Lancashire mills, including Ellenroad, used a rope-drive system to transmit power from the steam engine to the machinery. Ropes were connected to grooved pulleys on the flywheel of a steam engine, and transmitted the power to shafting on each floor. This method was first introduced to factories in Belfast during the 1850s. Very quickly it became the principal power system in Lancashire cotton mills. Rope-drive was used in other industries too, from brick works to iron-rolling mills.

The Ellenroad mill closed and was demolished – apart from the engine house and boiler house mentioned above – in 1985. In 1986 the Ellenroad Trust acquired the Whitelees beam engine and then in 1992 put it into steam. This engine has remained unchanged since it was first put to work in 1842, escaping the almost uniform practice of compounding that became the norm as boiler technology improved. The Whitelees engine was built by the Rochdale engine builders John Petrie and Company and is, in all respects, as James Watt left the steam engine when his patent for the separate condenser ran out in 1800. The engine has a Porter governor, parallel motion above the working cylinder and a flywheel with peripheral gear teeth for providing the drive.

The steam for the engines at Ellenroad was obtained from the single remaining Lancashire boiler, still coal-fired and one of five that originally powered the cotton mill. The need for more steam for bigger and better engines like these at Ellenroad was met by the efforts of a man called William Fairbairn in Manchester. In 1844 he made the Cornish boiler much bigger in diameter and, instead of having one fire tube through it, he put in two fire tubes, one by the side of the other. Coal was shovelled into underfeed stokers up to the furnace beds. Draught from the fans and the chimney supplied the air and the resulting hot gases passed through the furnace tubes to the back of the boiler. They were then drawn underneath the boiler and to the front where they divided and passed along both sides of the boiler, into the main flue and out of the chimney.

Four of the great Lancashire boilers at Ellenroad would be in steam at any one time, with one in reserve or being repaired. Each worked at

160 lbs per square inch (11 kg per cm^2) and together they could gobble up as much as 100 tons of coal every week. The beauty of these boilers was that you could burn anything in them. All of the soot fell to the bottom. The fires in them were so big and it took so long to get the steam up that they were only ever allowed to go out for one week in every year when all the mill workers went on holiday. Those who couldn't afford to go away had to go down in the flues with shovels and buckets and remove all the soot in readiness for when everybody came back from Blackpool and New Brighton. The Black Gang, as they were called, only got a meagre pittance for this filthy work, and when they'd got the job done they'd go to the pub and get inebriated. Then everything was ready for lighting the boiler again so it could carry on for another twelve months.

The take-up of the Lancashire boiler was rapid and it was soon being exported all over the world. There are pictures of Lancashire boilers being loaded up to be sent to India and Russia – all made in Lancashire. One of the reasons for this boiler's popularity was that it was very economical. It worked off natural draught, which is why 200-foot (61-m) factory chimneys were built. The wind would blow across the top of the chimney, and air would be sucked in through the two fire tubes in the boiler and this made the thing go.

In the second half of the nineteenth century steam power became the driving force for the major public utilities of water and electricity. As the Industrial Revolution had developed, new challenges had arisen. A rapidly growing population together with the development of new industries and the expansion of older ones produced a rapidly increasing demand for water for domestic and industrial requirements. This increased demand for water, combined with an awareness that a plentiful supply of pure water was essential to the health of the people, led to parliamentary legislation for the supply of water. As well as getting clean water into the cities, there was also the problem of removing waste. Yet again, steam power was the key, providing the power that brought the fresh water in and took the sewage out.

During the Victorian age things were built bigger than ever before and a perfect symbol of the time was London's Tower Bridge: a massive feat of engineering. The nineteenth century had seen the population of

London's East End grow so rapidly that a downstream crossing over the River Thames was needed. The major problem the engineers had was how to construct a bridge while allowing ocean-going vessels to continue using the Port of London – the largest and wealthiest port of the age. A public competition was held in 1876 to produce a design, but it wasn't until 1884 that Horace Jones, the city architect, provided the answer by coming up with his plan for a bridge built on the bascule (see-saw) principle of a lifting central section which, when raised, would leave a space 200 feet (61 m) wide through which even the tallest ships could pass. Steam was the power that would make all this possible.

The bridge, which was first opened in 1894, took eight years to build – twice as long as had been originally estimated. The project involved the labour of around 430 construction workers, ten of whom lost their lives while working on the bridge. Two gigantic piers had to be sunk into the riverbed to support the construction. What you can see now on the outside is a granite and Portland stone 'cladding', designed to make the bridge harmonize with the Tower of London, near which it stands, but the bridge is actually built from 11,000 tons of steel and it is incredibly strong. When completed, Tower Bridge was the largest and most sophisticated bascule bridge ever built. It was

Above: London's Tower Bridge. Steam power was used to raise and lower the bascules until 1976.

opened by the Prince and Princess of Wales on 30 June 1894 and all along the royal route and the banks of the river crowds of Londoners and visitors from all over the world arrived for a glimpse of the grand occasion. There was so much excitement and applause after the royal salute that it drowned out the Bishop of London as he attempted to bless the great construction. In its first month of operation the bridge was opened 655 times – 30 per cent more than in a whole year today.

Outwardly its appearance has changed little in the past hundred years, but the steam-driven engines, which raised and lowered the bascules, were replaced in 1976 with an electric and hydraulic system. The steam-powered machinery is still there though, and you can take a tour of the bridge and see it in its original engine rooms. The boiler room houses two of the gigantic Lancashire boilers which provided the steam at 75 lbs per square inch (5.3 kg per cm^2) to power the 360-horsepower (269-kw) pumping engines, which you an also see. The pumping engines in turn pumped water into the hydraulic system at 750 lbs per square inch (53 kg per cm^2). Six 100-ton accumulators stored this reserve of power (pressurized water) and maintained the pressure at 750 lbs per square inch (53 kg per cm^2). As the pressurized water was fed in, each accumulator would rise 35 feet (10.7 m) into the air on its great piston. The power was stored and used to raise each 1,200 ton-bascule carrying a counterweight of 350 tons on demand. Although the system may seem quite complex, the bascules could be raised to their maximum 86 degrees in about a minute.

When shipping on the Thames was at its peak, Tower Bridge would be opened at any time of the day or night, to allow vessels to pass. Today at least twenty-four hours' notice has to be given and a precise time arranged. One of the original eight bascule engine drives is still on display in the engine house. Each of these three-cylinder engines converted the hydraulic power to move the drive shaft and pinions, which interlocked with massive toothed quadrants on each bascule and raised and lowered each side of the enormous bridge. In 1952 a London bus had to leap from one bascule to the other when the bridge started to rise with the bus still on it! The engineering was to such a high standard that the modern machinery at Tower Bridge still uses the original drive shafts.

By the end of the nineteenth century the use of steam power was at its peak and there can't have been a branch of transport or industry that wasn't reliant on steam. Because of this great variety of uses there was a vast range of steam engines of all sorts and shapes and sizes in use all over the world, from the beam engine that was still going up and down at water-pumping stations, to great horizontal single-cylinder ones, to cross-compound ones and four-cylinder ones and all kinds of permutations. A man called J. A. Ewing catalogued them all in terms of their design in his manual *The Steam Engine* in 1894. In general they were of the 'reciprocating or piston-and-cylinder type', but they could be classified in several different ways.

Condensing engines reuse their steam by cooling it back to water to be reused by the boiler. This saves on fuel and heat. The condenser is a vessel into which the exhaust steam goes instead of going out into the atmosphere up the exhaust pipe. So the heat from the steam is put back to good use again. Non-condensing engines do not reuse their steam, but send it out into the atmosphere, as seen in early steamboats and steam railroad locomotives. A non-condensing engine is very un-economical. Many pit-winding engines were non-condensing because they had such high pressure. The exhaust steam, after it's done its work in the cylinders, just disappears up the exhaust pipe up to heaven and rains down on the neighbourhood in the form of dew. So all the steam condenses in the atmosphere instead of in a chamber.

To get even more economy out of the pressure of the steam that issued from the boiler the compound engine was invented. John McNaught of Bury was a key figure in this field, adding a high-pressure cylinder to a Watt engine at the opposite end to the low-pressure cylinder. The basic working principle of a compound engine is that there would be a high-pressure cylinder of a fairly small diameter that would perhaps get 150 lbs per square inch (10.5 kg per cm^2) going on to the piston. When the high-pressure cylinder had used that steam to push the piston one way, instead of exhausting into the atmosphere, went into an expansion chamber. By this time it had lost some of its power through expansion, so it went into the low-pressure cylinder, which was much bigger in diameter. As time went by engines were developed in which the steam condensed three or four times until it actually got to the far end where they had an enormous piston. This was almost at atmospheric pressure – so they got every ounce of energy out of that steam that they could possibly get. This gives us a further classification of compound engines according to the number of stages: double, triple or quadruple expansion engines. Compound engines were more efficient than simple ones, and triple expansion engines became the backbone of the shipping industry.

Another way of classifying engines is according to whether they are single- or double-acting. The distinction between them depends on whether steam acts on one side only or on both sides of the piston. In double-acting engines the steam both pushes and pulls the piston, but in single-acting engines, such as Newcomen's, the piston moves back due to atmospheric pressure rather than the pressure of steam.

The position of the cylinders is another element for categorization. They can be horizontal, vertical or inclined. Most vertical engines have the cylinder set above the crankshaft. The horizontal engine became the most popular of the 'beamless' type in Britain but not until the 1850s, perhaps because of the cost of replacing beam engines. Another way of classifying engines is according to where they worked, so we have stationary, locomotive and marine engines. Locomotive, marine and some kinds of stationary engines, such as those in heavy rolling mills, are 'reversing', which means they have a valve mechanism to allow them to run either way.

Towards the end of steam-engine development technology became very advanced. An important development was the invention of new valve gears in America. George Henry Corliss invented one resembling four gas taps, one on each corner of the cylinder. When the eccentric rod went one way it pushed and opened the gas tap on that corner and the steam went in, and when it went back the other way it opened the tap on the bottom corner and the exhaust and the steam went out.

The very last development was the uni-flow engine. This always seemed very modern to me. There was one at a tannery in Bolton and it was all enclosed – you couldn't see anything going round and yet it ran beautifully. I know that when they smashed it up it had run for forty-odd years without breaking down; and this was day and night, not just every hour or two. All they had to do every holiday was just put a few new packings in it and it kept going.

And now this brings me to a very important part of steam history: safety – or the lack of it! Boiler explosions were common, especially in the first fifty years. Several things caused explosions – corrosion, furring, clumsy repairs, low water level causing firebox plates to overheat. Trevithick was the first to design a lead plug, which would melt if the firebox crown overheated. Steam is dangerous because of its properties of expanding with unbelievable volume. These expansive properties are the secret really. As an example, if I were to turn on the steam in my own steam engine and fill the pipe up with steam and then turn off the stop valve, the amount of steam that's just contained in the pipe, by acting as a receiver for it, could keep the engine going for ages after I've turned off the stop valve. It's incredible what power it has.

Somewhere in my collection of photographs I have a wonderful picture of a weaving-shed steam engine that's actually run out of control and blown itself to pieces. If you experiment with a model of a steam engine, you can get it batting round at an unbelievable speed when all the connecting rods and the crankshaft are just a blur and you cannot see the spokes in the flywheel. But if you tried that with a full-size steam engine, say a 500- or 600-horsepower (370- or 450-kw) engine, they just couldn't stand the pressure. The flywheel would disintegrate, all the connecting rods would end up bent and everything would be a terrible mess. This was what happened to the weaving-shed engine in my photograph.

The tale starts one day when this thoroughly modern news-paperman came to see me with his photographer. The photographer was getting on a bit and he said, 'When I was a lad and I worked for the *Chorley Guardian*, the editor said, "Get yourself off to such-a-body's weaving shed. There's been an explosion." So I set off down the road with my camera to this weaving shed to be greeted by an unbelievable scene of carnage and disaster. The roof had been ripped off the engine house and the ropes were thrown away hanging over what was left of the walls, and the fire brigade with their big tall hats on were present. What had happened was that all the machinery and the line shafting in the weaving shed had started going round at 1,000 miles an hour

(1,610 kmph) and everything was shaking. The whole works looked as though it was going to fall down. The governors on the engine had gone wrong and the engine was building up revolutions, going really, really fast. There were two men in the engine room at the time and one of them said, "I'll go and get the women out of the weaving shed. You go and see the engineer about getting the engine stopped." The guy who was going to the engine house was halfway across the yard when the whole thing blew. He copped his lot and ended up dead. But the man in charge of the engine was turning off the stop valve. He had just got it down to 'shut' when the almighty explosion happened, so all he suffered was a broken arm and he survived. But bits of the engine were going through *Coronation Street*-type rooftops 500 yards (457 m) down the road.' That was quite late on, probably in about 1956. It must have been one of the last-steam driven weaving sheds in Chorley.

Here in Bolton there were disasters that my Dad used to tell me about. There was one in Lever Street at a mill with a wonderful name – Cross and Winkworths. The engine ran away there and the flywheel disintegrated, taking the end out of the engine house. It danced across the mill yard in bits and pieces, and seven-eights of it went in the mill lodge and disappeared from sight completely under the water. It's probably still there. There were a lot of disasters in the olden days. To be an engine driver or an engine 'tenter', as they were referred to in Lancashire, was a very responsible business. You might look through the window and see the guy sitting there in an easy chair apparently half-asleep, but he'd be listening to the engine for any slight deviation in the noise that was drumming on all day in his head. If it just made a few little funny noises, he had to find out what it was, because they couldn't afford to stop it. If the engine stopped, it was a disaster in two ways: not just from the management point of view, but for the workers as well, because they weren't earning any money. Nobody liked the engine minder if the engine stopped.

A lovely story springs to mind about an engineer's assistant and it is quite sad, really. At one time I was working at a mill called the Aron mill in Oldham. I've always been a bit of a magpie and was rooting in the bins when I found this beautiful leather-bound ledger. On the front

Left: My great hero Isambard Kingdom Brunel, the versatile engineer who constructed the Great Western Railway.

Below: Brunel and the Great Western company were rebels. While the other companies adopted Stephenson's 4-foot-8½-inch (1.5 m) gauge, Brunel decided that his railway would be 7-foot-¼-inch (2.1 m) which allowed greater speeds. If they still used that gauge today, our trains would be bigger and faster.

Below: The Great Western line was going to begin at Euston but Paddington station was constructed and opened as it's terminus. in 1838.

Overleaf: At the National Railway museum in York you can see one of my favourites – Patrick Stirling's beautiful *No 1* locomotive built in 1878.

Previous page: The London and North Eastern Railway's *Mallard* which did 126 miles an hour between Grantham and Peterborough – a steam record that has never been broken. You can see this at the National Railway museum, too.
Above: The beam engine at Middleton Top Engine House in Derbyshire pulled wagons up an incline on the Cromford and High Peak Railway.

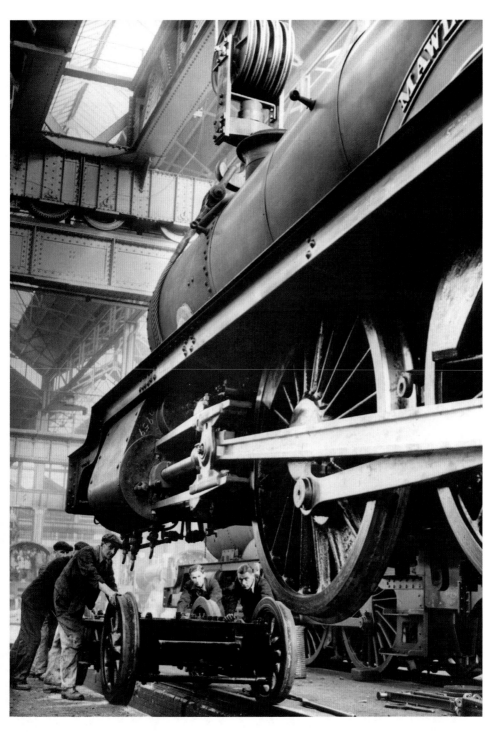

Above: Brunel's wide gauge was scrapped in the 1890s but the Great Western line expanded and grew. Many fine standard gauge locomotives were built at the company's Swindon works.

Left: Raising steam on an LMS Railway Class 5 engine in 1936. Below: By the 1930s the Great Western was one of the largest and most successful railway companies in the world and its gleaming Brunswick-green locomotives had familiar names known in homes throughout the country. The excitement and appeal of steam trains is well illustrated in this *Speed to the West* poster produced in 1939. It shows a 'King' class locomotive driving a holiday train bound for the west country. You can catch a glimpse of the golden age of the Great Western Railway by visiting Steam – the Great Western Museum in Swindon and the Didcot Railway centre.

GWR SPEED TO THE WEST GWR
CORNWALL DEVON SOMERSET WALES

of it in embossed gold were the words 'The Engine Statistics Book. Aron Mill. Oldham. 1905'. I opened it up to see beautiful copperplate writing in ink describing the commissioning of the engines such as: '...the left-hand side's named after Dorothy, one of the Director's daughters, and the right-hand side's named after another Director's daughter and major such-a-body turned it on...'. The ledger went on until the days when they started having a bit of bother. It said: 'June 4th 1907. Wainwright's fitters came today and repacked high-pressure piston rod...', and that's about it. They had five boilers and there was always one out of commission for the boiler inspector to come and have a look at and it's even got his name and his comments in the book. The boilers would be pretty new, so there wouldn't be a lot to do – just maybe a valve wanted fixing or something. One day in 1919 the ledger recorded: 'Wainwright's fitters came today and took away high-pressure piston rod and took a skim off it and new glands for the engine...' Every revolution of the engine every day was recorded in this book, how many tons of coal were burned every week and how many tons of coal were in stock in the mill yard. I then found something quite funny. It said: 'April 23rd. New engineer's assistant started today; Enoch Butterworth.' On the 24th: 'New engineer's assistant knocked unconscious by crank pin.' It was clear that he'd got too close to these big lumps going round and one of them had hit him on the head. 'June 25th. Enoch Butterworth off sick'! The ledger goes on like this and the years roll by. During the bad times in 1930, the writing begins to go downhill a bit; it doesn't have the same quality. Then in about 1952 it changes from ink to pencil. It just says, '60 tons of coal on stock in mill yard, 28,000 gallons (127,291 litres) of fuel oil...' with no mention of the demise of the steam engine, which of course must have been smashed up. By this time they had gone on to doing the heating system by fuel oil and then the ledger entries come to an end. It is all very sad in a way. But poor Enoch Butterworth – BANG!

Because they could be such dangerous things, steam engines began to be heavily tested by insurance companies and banks of engineers with indicators who did graphs of how much steam was pushing the piston up and down. You can buy these steam-engine indicators at car boot sales today and there are literally hundreds of them. Every boiler inspector in the land had one. He would go to a mill and put his steam indicator on the engine, a bit like a doctor with a stethoscope. They are lovely things, very beautifully made. A wonderful book I have called *Red Hot Furnace Crown Experiments* describes how, during the 1870s in Manchester, William Fairbairn tried to prove once and for all that squirting cold water into a red-hot boiler didn't make it blow up.

For the experiment he used a full-size Lancashire boiler, 30 feet (9 m) long and 8 feet (2.4 m) in diameter with two 3-foot (90-cm) fire tubes, and they dug a big trench in a field nearby and built a bunker round and a block house. There were no fancy electronics then, but they had it all controlled with pulley wheels and wires and everything, which they operated from a safe distance. They made it so they could lower the water in the boiler below the top of the fire tubes and let them become red hot. They had wires through stuffing boxes on top of the boiler braced to hooks on top of the fire tubes. So, when it got red hot and the steam pressure began to shove down the crown of the firebox, they knew from graphs and rulers in their bunker exactly where the crown of the fire tube was in relation to the rest of the boiler. Because there was no welding then, the plates would be wrenched where the rivets were and of course the boiler would leak profusely. The experimenters allowed freezing-cold water on the red-hot plates many times to prove that you could not blow up a boiler in this way. Some of the eminent engineers of the time believed that it flashed it into steam too quickly for the safety valves, but this was proved not to be the case. The pressure does go up just a few pounds, but the cooling effect of the cold water on the plates puts it all to nothing again. It stays pretty well the same. It is rather frightening when you get a boiler with a lot of pressure on and you don't know where the water level is and you're tempted to put more water in it, but you think that there could be a catastrophe if you did. However, it is proved with theory and practice that the boiler does not blow up.

Even so, there were plenty of disasters. In 1862 at Hartley Colliery, Northumberland, a clean break in the beam of the pumping engine caused one of the worst steam accidents ever seen. When the beam snapped the broken half plunged down the only shaft, trapping 202 men and boys who gradually suffocated. After this, all pits were required by law to have at least two shafts. Not many boilers blow up these days, but when it happened in the olden days it'd completely dismantle the boiler room. Everything disappeared – the windows, the roof and the men who were standing beside it. It was nearly always the boiler man who got blamed for low water in the boiler. The Board of Trade would carry out inquiries after an accident like this and they always deemed it was low water that caused the collapse of the boiler, the flue tube and so on.

In Britain's industrial heyday steam provided the power for just about every industry, including steel manufacture. In Kelham Island Industrial Museum, beside the River Don in Sheffield, working machinery tells the story of the city's steel industry over the last 400 years, and here you can see what must be one of the biggest stationary steam engines in the world. The Don valley engine was used to provide the power to drive a rolling mill in one of Sheffield's steel works.

And there's a pit near my home at Astley Green where they have an engine that is definitely worth going to see. The pit itself has been closed for years now, but a lot of it has been left standing and there's a group of enthusiasts who are trying to restore the pithead machinery. What a task they face, though. I know how much time it takes for me to try to get my own steam engines done, but a whole pit – well, that's something else. The huge winding engine at this pit was built by Foster, Yates and Thorn in 1911 and it's very photographable. When you look at it, it's the perfect colliery picture. It's just a pity there aren't any ropes on it; that makes a difference. The shaft at Astley Green was 800 yards (732 m) deep and the engine was a four-cylinder compound engine with a drum that the ropes go round weighing 100 tons.

It's twenty years now since the mine was shut and at one stage it was a very sorry sight because there wasn't a complete pane of glass left in the engine-room windows and, with it being high up, the rain just went straight in at one side and out the other. The engine inside had just turned to red rust. Now, however, thanks to the work of enthusiasts, it's almost ready to run. They've got a Lancashire boiler for it and they have a grand collection of bits and pieces. They've got the wheels going round now, but they don't really do anything. They've also got a steam hammer, which I've had a bit of a play with, and about five or six steam engines, all connected up to a big vertical boiler. It's similar to the one I have, but it's a lot bigger. The pipe work they've got is so long that everything works hydraulically with lots of water coming out of pipes all over the place. They also have a circular saw, which they use for sawing up palettes to fire the boiler and keep the whole thing going. Then they have a nice display of mining memorabilia in what used to be the office.

There is a little winding engine made by John Woods, but you can't get near the top of the pit for railings and safety wire. This reminds me of an interesting tale concerning the shaft at Astley Green, about a miner who was doing some work on the shaft when he fell off the top of the cage. By pure chance he landed on top of the other one that was coming up just as the two cages were nearly level in the middle of this 800-yard-deep (732-m) shaft. Lucky, eh! But they reckon he never went down again.

In my collection of mining books there are some fine photographs of the big winding engine at Astley Green being put up. It's so huge they must have built the engine house around it. And I've got a picture of the men who did the job, all standing there big-capped and very proud. When they'd done it, those men must have had an unbelievable sense of satisfaction as they watched the engine go round. There were sixteen Lancashire boilers in a row that drove it all and the poor lads that are struggling there now have only one package boiler not that much bigger than the one I've got.

CHAPTER FOUR

STEAMING DOWN THE ROAD

A traction engine is a strange sort of machine that has gone out of fashion now. It was developed from a lot of other engines and it started off not in urban industrial areas, but on the land, in the country of all places, where all the effort was put in either by animals or human beings. To begin with, the earliest traction engines were all adapted portable engines, with the cylinders over the firebox and chain drive. At first, the steering was done by horses, later by a steersman on the front of the engine, and then it progressed to the system we know today. Different makers had different ideas as to which side the steering should be situated, right or left.

The portable was the first type of steam engine to be used on and around farms in Britain. It was not self-propelled and needed to be pulled by horses. The men in the country, the blacksmiths and village mechanics, decided that they would get a small locomotive boiler and place it on four wooden wheels with a pair of horse shafts at the front to move it from place to place. On top of it they put a small single-cylinder steam engine, which enabled it to drive a wide variety of machinery by endless belt. It could be used to drive threshing machines and big saws, and they were still in use well into the twentieth century. On farms, portables could be used to drive an infinite variety of machines. As well as ploughs and threshing machines, early milking machines and crop driers took their power from portables, as did a variety of crushers, cutters and pulpers.

In Victorian and Edwardian days the portable engine became the universal provider of transportable power. It was used on construction sites for driving pumps, mortar mills and mixers; in quarries for working crushers; in sawmills for powering saws and planers; in brickyards for turning pugmills; and in joiners and other workshops for driving overhead line shafting. In fact, there can have been few types of medium-sized machine capable of operation by an endless belt that were not, at some time or another, paired up with portables. This went on for some time until production ceased in the late 1930s with the development of the petrol-paraffin tractor, which was less costly to operate, but portable steam engines were still in use into the 1950s. Firms like Marshall's at Gainsborough in Lincolnshire were making them right up till the 1940s for export to South America for the sugar-beet works.

Agricultural general-purpose engines were the most common types to be seen around the countryside. They were basically used as a mobile power plant for threshing, tree pulling and general farm duties. All early threshers were stationary engines very much like the sort of engines used in a mill or a mine, but the first portable thresher appeared in the 1840s, and from then on this type rapidly replaced the fixed sort. These were not generally owned by the farmers themselves, but were operated by contractors touring from farm to farm.

Road locomotives were designed for heavy haulage on the public highways. They were usually larger than the normal traction engine and were fitted with three-speed gearing as opposed to two-speed in most traction engines. They were also sprung on both front and rear axles. An extra water tank was fitted under the boiler so that greater distances could be travelled between water stops. These were very powerful traction engines capable of pulling loads of up to 120 tons. Showmen's engines, though highly decorated and adorned with brass, fall into the category of road locomotive. Apart from hauling fair rides from one venue to another, they were also used for generating the power for the rides and for lighting.

Steam tractors were built as small road locomotives and were operated by one man, provided the engine was less than 5 tons in weight. They were used for general road haulage and in particular by the timber trade. The most popular steam tractor was the Garrett 4CD. Road rollers are perhaps the best known of all steam traction engines and they were working into the 1960s. The early rollers tended to be very heavy; even one weighing 30 tons was built. But it was soon discovered that weight alone did not make the best roller. 12 or 15 tons was the most favoured. With the introduction of Tarmac, rollers became even lighter, and some of the smaller ones weighed as little as 3 tons.

Ploughing engines were the largest of all the traction engines. They were worked as a pair or set. The engines themselves didn't run along the field ploughing; instead a cable spanning the field would be attached to each engine on a winding drum with a plough joined in the middle, which would be pulled up and down the field. One engine was built to pull on its right hand side, the other on its left, so they were referred to as right-hand or left-hand engines, though the positions were the reverse when working. These engines weighed around 22 tons each and could plough up to 30 acres (12 hectares) a day.

In addition to the six main groups there was also the steam wagon or lorry which was developed from the beginning of the twentieth century onwards. The first of these were 'overtypes', which had their engine mounted on top of the boiler in the same way as a traction engine. These engines were chain-driven and they were capable of speeds of up to 30 miles per hour (48 kmph). The designs included four- and six-wheelers, artics and tippers. By far the most popular builder of 'overtypes' was Foden of Cheshire. The 'undertype' wagon that followed was made with a vertical boiler with the engine mounted under the chassis, not unlike a modern lorry. Later models were fitted with pneumatic tyres and could reach speeds of 60 miles per hour (97 kmph).

Although the uses of the traction engine had become many and varied by the second half of the nineteenth century, the early development of steam vehicles to run on the roads was slow to get off the ground. Apart from the experiments by Cugnot, Murdock and Trevithick, the power of steam was not applied to the propulsion of vehicles for over a hundred years after it had first been used for raising water from mines. There were difficulties because the ordinary boilers were too heavy and it was hard to regulate the power to suit the terrain the engine was travelling on such as miry roads or getting up and down hills.

Steam power was first used in the agricultural industry in the early 1800s in the shape of the portable engine that had been developed by

Trevithick. It was used to drive threshing machines, saws and other farm machinery and was pulled around by horses. But it took the best part of another half-century to produce a portable engine that was light enough to be moved around a farm by a horse without running away or getting bogged down. One of the most successful developments of the portable engine for agricultural use was by Howden. The machine he developed was small, but it produced enough power for farms to run their machinery. He astounded farmers at the 1839 agricultural show in Lincolnshire with his impressive portable engine. Howden wanted to keep production of this engine at a low level in order to stop the countryside from being overstocked. But this early example of environmental concern didn't do him any good because, while he turned his attention elsewhere, other manufacturers followed his example and by the end of the nineteenth century, 30,000 working engines were in the countryside.

I always felt a bit sorry for the horse in front of the traction engine. The only way of steering the thing was still the old tried-and-tested way of pulling a wagon; that is, by putting a pair of horse shafts at the front with a cart horse in between them. If the chap with the regulator (the tap that makes the steam work the engine) got a bit out of hand, accidents could happen. Noone ever actually recorded if there were any terrible disasters like running over the horse or the horse losing its feet or anything like that, but there must have been a few unfortunate old Dobbins who met a fairly violent death.

However, they couldn't go on forever with horses pulling steam engines around the fields. The logical development of the horse-drawn portable engine was the traction engine, which could not only drive machinery, but could also get around the farm under its own steam and haul other pieces of machinery around. The pioneers in the field of traction-engine development were the firm of J. R. and A. Ransome of Ipswich, which was established in 1789.

Robert Ransome was born in 1753, the son of a Norfolk schoolmaster. He was apprenticed to an ironmonger in Norwich and soon opened his own business and acquired a small iron foundry. In 1841 his first portable engine was exhibited at the Royal Agricultural Show in Liverpool. It was a historic moment, although few of those attending probably realized this. A year later he demonstrated an engine at the Royal Agricultural Show in Bristol, which was driven by a chain connecting the crankshaft and the wheels. This was his first self-propelled engine. Even so, a horse was still needed for steerage. In 1849 Ransome's thought they had provided the answer when they exhibited their 'Farmer's Engine' at the Royal Agricultural Show in Leeds. It was transportable under its own power and it was the first time in the history of steam that no horse was needed for steerage. Bevel wheels, operated from the driving position, turned the wheels in the direction required. But still it failed to become universally acknowledged. It is said that it was the nature of the times to be reluctant to change.

Not only were Ransome's the pioneers of steam locomotion in agriculture, but they also manufactured road locomotives. The road steamers had barely been tried and tested when the Indian government bought one, with a view to test its use for passengers and goods. It was proved that the rubber tyres that were fitted were not affected by the climate and, on the whole, the experiments were so satisfactory that four larger, high-speed road steamers were ordered. At this time Ransome's led the way in making a name for British engines abroad. The first completed engine, *Chenab*, was sent by road from Ipswich to the Royal Agricultural Show at Wolverhampton in 1871. The Indian

Above: Ransome and May traction engine, 1849.

government stipulated that the engines had to be able to travel several hundred miles towing a load. The trial was a success as far as the engine and tyres were concerned, but the boiler failed as it couldn't be kept steam-tight. Further tests were carried out on a run to Stafford. Again the boiler caused problems and it is reported that it had to be treated with red lead and oatmeal to stop the leaks. The engine had to be stopped continually to raise steam and on the return journey the copper blast nozzle was melted off, totally disabling the engine. The second engine built for the Indian government, *Ravee*, gave excellent results and the Indian locomotives were used for carrying mail and passengers between two stations in Punjab, about 70 miles (113 km) apart.

Back in England John Fowler, in Leeds, had grand ideas about ploughing by steam. He was one of the first to see the potential of developing a small, portable steam engine for use in agriculture and he manufactured some of the first steam-powered ploughs and threshing machines. During a period of more than thirty years he made the construction and use of traction engines his special study, and carried out the most extensive and exhaustive experiments regardless of the expense.

Fowler was born in Wiltshire in 1826, the third son of a wealthy Quaker merchant, and he might well have lived longer and more comfortably had he followed the business of a corn merchant, as his father had wished. But he gained valuable experience in farming methods, which was to be particularly useful later when he went on to become a pioneer of mechanized agriculture. It was after seeing the famine in Ireland following two years of failed potato crops that he gave up his job, determined to mechanize land drainage by the use of steam. The result was his mole drainage plough, shown in London at the Great Exhibition of 1851, and built for him by Ransome's. This 'mole drainer' was a great, shell-shaped piece of iron with a knife on it. They stuck it down into the ground and dragged it by brute force through the clay. It cut a slot in the clay and left a round hole down below, which created drains under heavily clayed land. In 1858, Fowler was awarded the £500 prize offered by the Royal Agricultural Society of England for his balance plough. He was said to have spent ten times the amount of the award on his experiment to produce it. His first successful ploughing engine was built for him by the firm of Clayton and Shuttleworth at their works in Lincoln. Sets of ploughing tackle were built for him by several contractors until he set up on his own in the 1860s in Leeds.

Fowler was highly successful in introducing pairs of traction engines standing one on each side of a field. The earliest ploughing engines were weird things – basically a portable engine with a great winding drum under the boiler. They were driven by gearing from the crankshaft and an endless wire rope going all the way round a field supported by anchors, which had big bobbins for the rope to pass round. Each one was equipped below the belly of the machine with a huge revolving drum, which could take up to 800 yards (732 m) of metal rope. Each engine pulled in turn to draw a simple plough across the field. At the end of each line the plough was lifted out of the soil

Above: Fowler's steam engine and windlass, 1862.

and a second one put in before that was dragged back across the field in the opposite direction. It must've taken a long time to set one of these things up and it needed a lot of men. The Fowler system made it possible to plough more deeply than had been possible before without compressing the soil with heavy wheels. The trouble was that the engines were expensive to buy and fuel costs were high, but the results were impressive.

Early on the ploughing engines had no steering gear. Instead, a pair of shafts was fixed to the front of the engine, and the machine was guided by good old-fashioned horse power. But farmers soon demanded a change to the nuisance of having a horse involved when they had paid a lot of money for all this new steam technology. So the ploughing engine was given its steering. Steam ploughing was a revolution in its time. It was reckoned at the time that a man and two horses, working a fifty-four hour week, would plough an acre a day. But with steam power, using two engines, five men and a watercart boy, plus a horse for pulling the watercart, the average was 15 acres (6 hectares) a day.

Fowler made his name from developing machines for ploughing but, following his untimely death in 1864 in a hunting accident at the age of thirty-eight, natural evolution determined that the company would look for other uses for steam traction. As roads improved, self-moving engines were developed and the traction engine as we know it was born. Apart from road haulage and timber work, the foremost employment of the traction engine was threshing. The characteristic engine of the very early years of threshing was 8-horsepower (6-kw), single- or double-cylindered. As boiler pressures increased, the 7-horse-power (5.2-kw) engine became popular. This was big enough to be capable of doing the work that was required, but not so big as to be awkward in the average stockyard. The disadvantages were that the engines were expensive to buy and fuel costs were high. Higher steam pressures and com-pounding of cylinders were introduced during the 1880s, which helped to reduce boiler size and economize on fuel and so cut running costs.

The coming of steam to the farm was a new experience and the look of the landscape began to change. Generally the ploughing and threshing was done by teams of engine-men brought in seasonally by agricultural contractors. Steam began to be applied to other uses on the land: drying grain, cooking animal food and, above all, drainage. The nineteenth-century drainage of the East Anglian Fens owed much to beam engines powering big scoop wheels.

When you've visited places like Lincolnshire, have you ever wondered about the size of those monster fields, all dead flat? I think most of that, apart from God's efforts in making the land reasonably flat, is the result of ploughing and cultivating. Ploughing was nearly all done by big companies that owned as many as twenty sets of ploughing engines. Forty engines must have been a lot of expense when you first bought them. But by 1918 or thereabouts the men who had a lot of these engines realized the advantages of the internal combustion engine and, of course, its lower cost. A big farmer could easily afford to buy one, and slowly but surely, steam ploughing got forced out.

But even until just before the Second World War steam-powered threshing machines working away in fields were still quite a familiar sight in the countryside. These seem very primitive when they are compared with modern combine harvesters, but they represented ingenious use of steam for agricultural purposes. The steam engine powered the threshing machine by a belt connected from the flywheel. Wheat, oats or barley were shovelled into the thresher at one end and went through rising and falling shafts, which separated the grain and discharged the straw at the other end. The grain passed through a number of sieves for grading and was finally discharged through three different holes where it was collected and sorted. The flywheel and belt also powered a spiked ramp, which carried the straw up to the top of the rick.

Even more successful than Fowler's were the steam traction engines developed by Thomas Aveling of Rochester. A traction engine is basically a mobile steam engine that evolved from the crude stationary engines of the eighteenth century. Aveling first introduced simple chain drives in 1860 and his inventions took the traction engine to new levels of speed and sophistication. This created the prototype for the traction engine that was to stay in commercial use for almost a century. It earned Thomas Aveling the recognition of 'father of the traction engine'.

Thomas Aveling, a farmer in Kent, was born in Cambridgeshire in 1824 and was a pioneer in the application of steam power to ploughing, road haulage and driving agricultural machinery. It was he who introduced most of the technical innovations that are incorporated in every 'modern' traction engine and steamroller. But nothing about his early life indicated the brilliance that would emerge; in fact, many considered him slow and dim-witted. This was largely down to his background. His father died shortly after he was born and his mother remarried a man who ruled him with a rod of iron. Aveling retreated into himself and it was only when he left home that his true character and abilities began to shine through.

He was apprenticed to a farmer in Cambridgeshire and it wasn't long before he started to demonstrate his skill in mechanics and engineering. He began by doing repairs for neighbours, but was soon looking for ways to make improvements. At the time the portable engine, transported by horses, was becoming established throughout the countryside as a source of power for various machines such as threshers. Aveling was not happy with this because of the hassle involved in moving it from site to site. He said it was an insult to mechanical science to see half-a-dozen horses dragging a steam engine along. He wanted to make the engines self-moving. Aveling's idea was to use the same power unit as the portable to provide traction. This was carried out successfully and the front wheels then replaced the horse. The engineer drove the machine to where it was needed for threshing corn, sawing timber, pulling down trees, pile driving, direct haulage of ploughing tackle and lifting huge blocks of stone for harbour works. But an animal was still needed to steer the machine. So Aveling was not yet finished.

He took out his first traction engine patent in 1859. At the time he didn't have the resources available himself, so he had to approach outside engine builders, such as the Lincoln firm of Clayton and Shuttleworth. By 1861 Aveling was in a position to start producing his own engines at his workshop at Rochester in Kent. One of the first problems he applied himself to in his new works was to find a way of getting rid of the horse that was still needed for steering his engine. He decided that if they put a dog clutch on the end of the crankshaft and a big sprocket on the back axle they could actually make the engine self-propelled. A lever was operated by a steersman who sat at the front. This was Aveling's 'pilot steerage', which was used for about six years until he developed the general traction engine into the form we recognize today.

As the traction engine developed, further improvements were made. The portable engine had the cylinder block over the top of the firebox, which is the hottest part of the engine, and the crankshaft supported on two brackets just behind the funnel at the front end. Now there was a problem here: the thrust of the connecting rods on the crankshaft, which was doing the driving, wrenched away at the studs that held the brackets to the boiler barrel at the coldest end of the boiler. As a result this would quite often cause horrible leaks. So Aveling, who was one of the great pioneers in traction-engine design, invented the 'horn plates'. He riveted two extra plates to each side of the firebox and formed a sort of box above the firebox that contained all the castings with the bearings in, the actual crank and some of the gearing that then went down to the back axle. This made the whole rear end of a traction engine very strong. It also enabled them to put a lot of nuts and bolts through the boiler to hold the cylinder block on, which meant that because there was a horizontal push it didn't spring as many leaks at the front end.

Another invention that Aveling came up with was the steam-jacketed cylinder. The steam leaving the boiler comes up through the bottom of the cylinder block and then goes right round the outer circumference of the cylinder into the stop-valve chest, which is the valve that controls the steam entering the valve chest proper. This kept the steam really hot and stopped it from condensing and washing away all the cylinder oil and the lubrication.

In 1862 Aveling went into partnership with Richard Thomas Porter. Porter was born in 1834, the son of a grocer in Sheffield. He is known to have provided the finance for their projects. Although not a wealthy man himself, he married Marian Atkins in 1861, and it is thought that she may have been from a wealthy family. Aveling and Porter devoted themselves almost exclusively to the manufacture of traction engines, ploughing engines and steam road rollers, and they were granted numerous patents. In 1864 one of their road engines named *El Buey*, which was made for the Traction Engine Company of Buenos Aires, hauled a load of 28 tons up Star Hill in Rochester – 305 yards (279 m) long, with an incline of 1 in 12. Early Aveling and Porter traction engines were 'chain engines', which used chains to drive the wheels rather than gears. The same basic design was used in road rollers and in chain-drive tram locomotives built during the 1860s. The design was quickly abandoned as technology advanced, but several hundred were built and sent all over the world. Out of all of these, only one is known to exist today. It is Aveling's 0-4-0 tram engine built in 1872, which you can now see at the London Transport Museum in Covent Garden.

Another of the great names in traction engines is Burrell. Charles Burrell and Sons of Thetford, Norfolk, were internationally acclaimed makers of steam engines and agricultural machinery. By the end of the 1800s they were exporting engines worldwide and had become one of the major employers in the area. They started to manufacture traction engines in 1856. Burrell was very inventive in his designs for road locomotives for different classes of work. Three of his first engines were sent to customers in Turkey. The engines had two cylinders, each with a 10-inch (25-cm) stroke. The boiler was of the 'pot' type, which gave a lot of trouble, so eventually he replaced it with the locomotive form of boiler and designed the engine to suit. The first of these was made for the Turkish government and was described as one of the best-designed road locomotives up to that time. The horizontal engine was placed on the top of the locomotive boiler, the cylinders near the firebox end of the boiler. It was all mounted on a wrought-iron frame and carried by four rubber-tyred travelling wheels. Similar and improved engines were sent to Greece and Russia for passenger services.

But, as innovative as Burrell and others were, I think it was Aveling who made the biggest contribution to the development of the traction engine. However, it depends really on how you look at it, because it's a bit like the development of the steam locomotive in that a lot of good ideas came from different people. There were basically two forms of traction engine: the four-shaft and the three-shaft. The four-shaft engine was favoured by John Fowler in Leeds and had much more complicated gearing than the three-shaft system. A good example of a three-shaft engine is one of those made by Burrell. This system basically uses a lot of cogs, like the ones in a big clock, connecting the crankshaft through the intermediate shaft to the back axle. It's debatable which is better, because on a four-shaft system all the gears that do the work are enclosed between framing and on a three-shaft engine they are on the outside so all the bearings and cogs hang over the wheels.

Towards the end of the nineteenth century traction engines got bigger and bigger. Heavy machinery needed to be moved all over industrial areas and a lot of it was too large for the loading gauge of the railways – for example, huge boilers, great steam accumulators, anvil blocks and, particularly awkward, the stern frames for big ships. All of these were made in places like Sheffield, but were assembled in Liverpool, Birkenhead and Glasgow. By the 1870s road locomotives were being made to pull very heavy loads like this. The average Lancashire boiler weighed about 30 tons and the traction engine was developed so that it would be strong enough to haul this sort of weight. Even this wasn't really adequate, as witnessed by old sepia photographs of locos with much more than 30 tons behind them struggling along the road. Quite often they had another engine behind to try to hold back the load, and the van that the haulers all lived in would be hitched on to that. There were disasters when the weight proved to be too much

Above: An Aveling and Porter traction engine circa 1880.

for the engines, especially as they rumbled down big hills and ended up in a ditch at the bottom with everything bent and broken.

The traction engine had a great impact on the world. Once this country had an almost boundless export market for them – North and South America, Canada, Australia, New Zealand, Russia. British-made traction engines were exported everywhere and won hundreds of medals and diplomas at exhibitions such as the Brussels Exhibition in 1872. In the Boer War they were sent to South Africa and there are pictures of them crossing rivers pulling great howitzers and if you study old photographs of the First World War, you'll see a lot of big guns at the front with traction-engine wheels. They must have gone round to every traction-engine manufacturer in the land and pur-loined as many wheels as they could to put on these guns.

Leeds was a great centre for traction-engine builders, being home to famous companies like the Yorkshire Steam Wagon Company and Mclarens. The biggest and best known was John Fowler. This firm made literally thousands of ploughing engines, road rollers and road loco-motives. Then just over the wall from John Fowler was Mclarens. There's a lot of jealousy in the world of traction engines and some say that the Mclaren road locomotives were made out of the bits that John Fowler threw over the wall. Another company, Marshall's, specialized in nice threshing machine engines and threshing boxes. Even to this day, if you're travelling in a train, you can see them, nearly always a pinky-red colour with 'Marshall' along the top, rotting away in the fields. Alas, Mr Marshall died about two or three years ago, but I remember chatting to him; one of the last in the line of a family who made traction engines for a living.

As well as powering machinery in the fields and providing the power for road haulage, portable and traction engines were used on travelling fairgrounds. Steam was first applied to the roundabout in about 1870 by Henry Soame of Mersham in Norfolk. He took the power from a portable engine by means of a flat belt drive. Frederick Savage of King's Lynn, also in Norfolk, became the leading manufacturer of portable engines adapted to drive fairground rides – a spin-off from his agricultural engine business. Out of this developed a special breed called the fairground engine or showman's road locomotive. The showman's engine was just a road locomotive covered with a lot of embellishments that hauled the showmen's caravans and trucks around the country. It was all beautifully tarted up with candyfloss twisted brass pillars and lots of ornamentation that wasn't on the heavy haulage engines. Its main embellishment was a great dynamo on the front that drove music machines and electric motors that drove swings and roundabouts and generated electric light. Fairground men have always been interested in the most modern things. Today they've all got little compact disc players and such like, making a hell of a row. In the olden days, with the great organs that were powered by their engines, they made as much noise then as they do now. The steam engine even worked its way into the early cinematograph days, when the showman's engine arrived and they used the engine to generate the electricity needed for a bioscope show. The engine would come with a dynamo and the projector and everybody would think it was a wonderful piece of tackle.

The showman's engine is a magnificent sight and they made them more and more beautiful and bigger and grander until the 1930s. But after the Second World War the market for them dried up, because in 1945 there were lots of old ex-American army heavy-haulage wagons around that had pulled tank transporters. Straightaway the fairground men jumped on to them and made the showman's engine obsolete; it just disappeared. By the late 1940s the scrapyards were full of derelict showman's engines in very sad condition and you could purchase one for a few hundred quid. Now, however, it would cost you over £300,000 to buy one. I think some of those fairground men wished they had kept their engine in the corner of a field somewhere.

For many people the traction engine must have been their first encounter with the 'machine age'. If they lived in the country, it would have been the first time they saw corn being fed on to a threshing machine that never stopped. Or they might have seen traction engines being used to haul heavy industrial equipment or to pull road trains of several wagons. They'd have plenty of time to watch them because they were very slow. Some people's first experience might have been when travelling on one of the early steam carriages.

Going back a bit before traction engines, there were many, many attempts to make steam-driven coaches for transporting people a long way by road. Road steamers had a lengthy history that stretched all the way back to Cugnot and his experiments in the 1760s and 1770s. In fact, steam carriages had been seen on the roads before traction engines came into general use on the farm. Following on from Trevithick's steam carriages in the early 1800s, Walter Hancock was one of the pioneers in this country. He devoted twelve years of his career to the development of steam carriages. In 1824 he invented a novel engine which was simple, light and comparatively cheap. He patented a boiler for a road engine as early as 1827, which was what made his steam carriages so successful. He proved that a steam carriage could travel up steep hills, which had been doubted by many.

Infant was one of nine steam carriages that Hancock built. In 1832 it ran from London to Brighton and back carrying eleven people at a speed of 9 miles per hour (14.5 kmph). In 1833 he built the *Autopsy* and the *Enterprise*. The *Autopsy* ran for hire daily for four weeks between Pentonville and Finsbury Square in London. It then ran along with the *Era* for four months in 1834 between the City and Paddington. During this period it carried nearly 4,000 passengers. Hancock was the only proprietor to operate a locomotive along the busy streets of London at peak times of the day. The *Era* was shipped to Dublin in 1835 to carry passengers on the streets there. At one time it reached a speed of 18 miles an hour (29 kmph). Hancock's coaches were reported to have been better than any others that were built over the next fifty years, but they stopped running. This is put down to the fact that he was a better inventor than commercial man, so after many years of effort he had to give up.

Another early steam carriage built in 1833 by Michael Roberts of Manchester saw the introduction for the first time of a differential gear. Roberts worked for an engineering firm called Sharp, Roberts and Company which built a road locomotive, subjected to a public trial in December 1833. There were a few imperfections, but it demonstrated the soundness of the principle on which it was constructed. On a second trip in March 1834, it carried forty passengers 1½ miles (2.4 km) along Oxford Road, Manchester, at up to 20 miles an hour (32 kmph). A month later, on another outing, it suffered an accident when the boiler burst on the streets of Manchester. It seemed that the pump on the engine didn't work properly and the water in the boiler was danger-ously low. Roberts was credited for inventing the differential gear, which he used on the company's engines. It's a device that superseded claw clutches, friction bands, ratchet wheels and other complicated arrangements to obtain the full power of both the driving wheels and at the same time allowing the engine to turn the sharpest corner without any difficulty. Sixty years later his arrangement was still being used on traction engines of the day. Roberts died in poverty in March 1864 at the age of seventy-five. He was described as having helped others but forgotten himself. Many profited from his inventions without even acknowledging his contribution.

At this stage in the development of the steam carriage there were a lot of complaints from the public and a strong anti-steam lobby grew. During the 1830s Hancock's steam carriages aroused animosity on the grounds that they created unpleasant smoke and frightened the horses. In 1831 the Red Flag Act was passed. This decreed that any damage done to the roads by a traction engine had to be paid for by the owner; whereas if damage was done by horses pulling an engine no one was liable. No traction engine was allowed on the public highway unless a man walked 60 yards (55 m) ahead carrying a red flag to warn other road users of the dangers. Locomotive acts in 1861 and 1865 kept down speeds in Britain to 2 miles an hour (3.2 kmph) in towns and 4 miles an hour (6.4 kmph) in the country. Decades passed before rules such as this were reversed. Steam carriages were badly let down by the poor state of the roads and the fact that they were disliked by turnpike men and stagecoach proprietors, who tried to sabotage them with tricks like putting piles of rocks in their path. The braking system on these carriages wasn't too good, so when there was a problem with the brakes one or two of them tipped over and there was a number of explosions, which didn't do a lot to encourage the public to travel on them.

But they were proving to be an efficient form of transport even though they never really took off in the way the railways had done. In September 1871 Burrell carried out some interesting trials at Thetford with two of his passenger locomotives. The large road engine weighing 10½ tons carried a load which brought it up to 37 tons. It drove through the streets at 5 miles an hour (8 kmph) and at one place climbed a hill with an incline of 1 in 18 without the slightest sign of any slipping. The engines drew a huge amount of attention and it was said that they proved there was no difficulty whatsoever in applying steam on common roads for the purpose of carrying passengers. But they still didn't really take off. In the early 1900s steam carriages were resurrected once again and steam-driven tram cars, which were quite wonderful things, were made. Nearly every major city in the world had steam-driven trams in a strange period in between horse-driven and electrically powered ones. They were nearly always in the form of a tractor that pulled what were, I suppose, ex-horse-drawn tram-car bodies on wheels behind them.

Possibly the best known of all steam engines built for the road is the steamroller, first made by Thomas Aveling. Its design used a very heavy flywheel that was quite different from anything used in chain-drive traction engines. Basically, they got a traction engine and put two cone-shaped rollers instead of front wheels on it, with a central pivot. The trouble with this idea was that the conical rollers had a nasty sliding effect. So they then developed a pair of front forks and two rollers for the differential movement on a dead axle through the bottom. The early rollers were built in collaboration with the inventor William Batho and are usually known as 'Batho rollers'. The best known Batho roller is *Aveling and Porter No. 1*, the famous 'Liverpool Roller', the first production road roller in the world, built in 1867.

Aveling's road rollers were used all over the world – two of them became the first steamrollers in the United States, helping on many major projects including the roads in New York's Central Park. Without the steamroller, roads could never have been made suitable for high-speed mechanically propelled vehicles. Every nation seemed to buy a British road roller, and photographs of foreign rollers show that they all had Fowler or Aveling similarities. It's as though they bought a Fowler or an Aveling, pulled it to pieces and then used all the bits to create a similar sort of machine.

Aveling and Porter continued to manufacture steamrollers until after the Second World War. Many remained in service well into the 1960s and today outnumber all other kinds of preserved steam engines.

All surviving traction engines, road locomotives and steamrollers are more or less based on the Aveling patents. It was Aveling's designs which made mechanical road transport possible and created the modern highways, which we take for granted today. The first properly made roads were just crushed-up stone, stone dust and water. If you ran over this with something really heavy, it consolidated it all. It was very good once it had had a lot of weight over it, but when it got wet and had borne the narrow wheels of horse-drawn carts, it soon got a bit rutted. The next type of road surface to be used was a coat of tar with pebbles or granite chippings thrown on top, which all dried on top in one layer. Every year they'd keep putting more and more of this on and it would end up resembling Tarmac. It was a scotsman called John Macadam who was responsible for a road-making revolution. He was born in Ayr in 1756 and made his fortune in his uncle's counting house in New York. Macadam returned to Scotland in 1783 and began experimenting with a new form of road construction. His new surface was simply a base of large stones covered with compacted stone and gravel, bound together with tar. The tar 'glued' all the stone together and made a harder, smoother surface for traction engines and carriage wheels. A raised camber in the middle meant that any water would

Above: Aveling and Porter's Liverpool steamroller, 1867.

drain off each side of the road. The new surface was called 'Tarmacadam roads' but it was a bit of a mouthful and gradually became shortened to 'tarmac'. Macadam was made surveyor-general of metropolitan roads in England. By the end of the nineteenth century most of the main roads in Europe were built in this way.

Asphalt came along much later. It was applied a lot more thickly, which made things difficult for the conventional steamroller. The modern yellow Edison machines you see along motorways today are diesel-rollers. Everybody still calls them steamrollers for some strange reason; it's a term that has never fallen out of use. When a conventional three-point steamroller with a flywheel going round and half a mile of gearing in between the back axle and the crankshaft needs to be put in reverse, the business of stopping and starting again is too long. The whole weight of the engine sinks into the asphalt. They even tried making steamrollers without flywheels – modernistic-looking machines called *Wallace and Stevens Advanced*. But it was too late by then and the diesel or petrol engine had taken over from the world of steam road rolling. However, steamrollers still had their uses. Even when the M1 motorway was being built in the mid twentieth-century, it is said that, at the start of the work, the ballast and the rough stuff underneath was rolled by steam engines.

The biggest collection of steamrollers and traction engines that I know of belongs to George Cushing of Norfolk. I first heard of Mr Cushing as quite a young man when my interest in steam engines first developed, and was intrigued that here was someone living deep in the country who had a field literally full of traction engines and steamrollers. In the village of Thursford, George Cushing has built up and restored a collection of showman's engines, fairground rides, pipe organs, steamrollers and traction engines to rival any in the world. As a young lad in 1920 he visited a steam fairground and was so amazed by these bright, gleaming engines powering rides and organs that he was determined to have an engine of his own. At first he scraped together all his pennies and bought a steam traction engine and worked as a contractor of sorts on the farms. One of his regular jobs was running sugar beet to the station with his traction engine, and he still has photographs of two of the surviving Aveling ploughing engines that he used to use. The seed of a passion for steam engines had been sown, and with the decline in their general use he started a collection in his own field. While most people were scrapping their engines and cutting them up, George went around buying them. Of course at the time people thought he was completely mad, but he started to repair and restore the engines after the Second World War and now he has this marvellous collection that anybody can go to see and experience.

George Cushing's collection began in his field and shed, but now there is a proper visitors' centre there in Thursford. The engines have all been restored and are quite magnificent. They all look like new and you can walk around and touch them and really get a sense of what they must have looked like working on the land and in fairgrounds all over the country in the golden age of steam. The very first engine George bought was an Aveling and Porter and, like me, he swears by them. He also has three colonial tractors, which are the same as the one I am restoring in my shed, and many others, including a bright-red Foden steam tractor and a Clayton steam wagon, which he bought second-hand in 1932 for only £10. The showman's engines and organs are really ornate, with carved figures and patterns. There is even a resident organist who plays away on the Wurlitzer. There is a Victorian roundabout too, which they reckon is the last of its kind anywhere. It is called the 'Gondola' because all the carriages are shaped like Venetian gondolas. It has a switchback engine, powered by electricity these days, which raises and dips the roundabout as it goes round, and you can go and have a ride on it.

The number of engines that George has managed to collect and repair is quite amazing. The collection really is a tribute to the great men who designed and worked them. It's also worth quite a lot of money these days. A traction engine that you could buy in the 1940s for the princely sum of £200 is now almost priceless. Prices have really sky-rocketed – for a decent genuine model you may have to pay around £150,000 and some are even worth about £500,000 today. Last time I spoke to George about one of my engines, he advised me it would be worth £50,000 when I'd finished it.

I've got two engines myself. There's my steamroller that I've had for years and my traction engine, which I'm still working on. When I was young I knew a man who bought a fairground engine and I often asked to play with the thing. But I wanted one of my own like you want your own toy. So, about thirty-odd years ago, I bought a steamroller and I was ripped off because I paid £175 for it and found out later that you could buy one at that time for about £60 by outbidding the scrapman. Anyway, time went by and this steamroller was an incredible wreck: the back wheels leaned in on each other, and if you went over a manhole cover the road wheel banged on the edge of the flywheel. All the gearing had been built up with electric welding and worn away again. The tender, the tank and the water tanks were full of pan washers and it leaked and made the most unbelievable noise you could imagine. In fact, that is probably partly why I'm deaf now. You could drive the thing for 20 miles (32 km) to the early Lancashire traction-engine rallies; then, coming back in the Land Rover, you couldn't hear its engine running. It wasn't even a new Land Rover, it was second hand, but it felt as if you were driving a Rolls-Royce because you couldn't hear it after you'd been deafened by the racket of the steamroller. So, painstakingly over a period of thirty years and two divorces, I slowly but surely made a new steamroller right from scratch.

The boiler was in a terrible state. It had a great weld under the front like the wart on an ash tree. When you got inside the firebox there were great globs of welding from one stay bolt to another and it frightened me. So I just pretended it wasn't there and carried on with the beautification of the steamroller. I put new lagging round the boiler, fitted a new funnel and painted it, adding decorative lines. As you work your way back on a traction engine you come to the most difficult bit: the gearing. Of course all this gearing was very worn. Luckily, back in my days of steeplejacking I had access to a lot of engineering works. I got a full set of blanks for the gearing from Hick, Hargreaves in Bolton for nothing and it only cost me £200 to put all the teeth on. What a difference that made. Instead of driving a mad machine you could now go along the road calmly and actually hold a conversation with whoever was with you on the footplate. I remember with all the old gearing, the lids on the oiler used to dance about as you went along the road. But when we put in these new gears they just stayed put and they didn't rattle. I also made a brand-new tender.

The engine looked magnificent – better than when it was new – but it still had this big wart under the boiler at the front and the firebox was still full of horrible weld and ready for blowing up.

One night I came home from a function somewhere with the steamroller and when I stopped outside our front door it was making a horrible whistling noise down in its belly. Just like the man I described earlier in the big mill engine house listening to his engine going round, you got used to noises even with a traction engine. I opened the fire-hole door and saw water gushing out of a crack and trying to put the fire out inside. The first thing to do was to get the water out of it, get the grinder out, grind through the crack and get the welder to weld it up, which I did.

After this I did a whole summer season with the engine, going here, there and everywhere. But I knew that I had to face up to the terrible surgery it needed. I won the cup that year for the best steamroller in the Lancashire traction-engine club and I was feeling quite proud of myself when my boiler inspector appeared on the scene. I said to him: 'I'm going to take the engine home now, pull it to bits and make a new firebox and a new front tube plate and a new boiler barrel.' He panicked and said: 'No, don't do anything until I've seen the superintendent of the insurance company.' It all got sorted out in the end. But the first thing needed was a new boiler barrel.

With a boiler barrel everything must be done by people who are used to making pressure vessels. I went to a works and they rolled me this piece of plate round and welded the seam. To check it they first of all have it x-rayed and I was actually present when they did it in their metal laboratory. I asked the man if the weld was all right and he said: 'Yes, there's nowt wrong with it. There's no cracks and no muck in it, no coolant cracks or owt like that. You might as well take it home and get on with it.' So I brought it back to Bolton and I drilled about ninety holes in it with a ratchet drill, which is the creation of the devil. It is really hard work compared with using a big power-driven drill. The phone rang and it was the boiler inspector and he said: 'I should hang fire a bit. The elongation on the weld metal is a few decimal points short of what it should be and we cannot accept this weld metal in the longitudinal seam.' The people who'd done the job for me were adamant that there was nothing wrong with it. They did work for the North Sea oil people and they got their radiographer in and their examiner and he also said there was nothing wrong with it. The Scottish Boiler Insurance Company and this company who'd done the job argued between themselves and it went on and on and on. In the end I said: 'What happens if I rivet it like they used to?' That was different, there are no tests on a riveted seam. The people who did it said if the insurance company was not satisfied they would grind all the weld out and re-weld it for nothing. But they wanted another £72 worth of examin-ation, which in those days, twenty-odd years ago, was too much money for me. So they said that I could rivet it and if it stood the pressure of the hydraulic test and if it stood the pressure when it was steamed and the holes were drilled at the right centres, they would accept it. It must have been a bit difficult for an insurance company, having a young man say to them: 'I'm going to make a new boiler in a shed in the back yard.' There are lots of people doing it now throughout the country and they all stick to the rules, you have to when you're making a boiler. The insurance company even argued about the pitch of the rivet holes. I had a manual from National Vulcan that recommended one thirty-second of an inch difference between the centres of the rivet holes and the ones that the insurance company wanted done. But Aveling's were a sixteenth the other way. So which do you pick?

I was a steeplejack, which is miles away from being a boiler-maker. But I was very lucky because, close to the railway town of Horwich, there were a lot of men still alive who had actually made boilers for locomotives. I had two good teachers who came to advise me. They were so old they couldn't really do anything themselves; they'd just tell me how to do it. You can read a million books on practical subjects like riveting, but there is a big difference between reading and having to do it yourself. I was fortunate that the skills of boiler-making were shown to me by these lovely old men, who smoked Capstan full-strength and coughed profusely all the time they were doing it.

When the new boiler was almost finished, it had to pass the hydraulic test, which meant that it had to be full of water and a hydraulic pump was used to pressurize it one-and-a-half times its normal working pressure under steam. I was sitting in the firebox and old Donald, who used to work for me, was sitting outside working the pump when along came our illustrious boiler inspector, who said: 'Its got a blob; a leaking rivet; not pouring out, just wet.' I said to him: 'What can we do about this?' And he replied: 'You could put a run of weld round it.' I thought: 'Well! We've made this entire boiler using the old-fashioned skills and ways and this guy tells me to put a weld round it now.' I didn't want to do that. He said: 'There's only one other way that you'll stop it and that's fill it up and empty it and let it rust.' So we had a problem.

We had just three weeks before we were due to go out on the road with the engine. They say necessity is the mother of invention, and after racking my brains until I thought they were going to explode, I came up with a solution – so simple and so easy. You get a piece of 3 x ½-inch (1.3-cm) bar and drill a 2-inch (5-cm) hole in the top of it about three sixteenths of an inch from the edge and put the hole over the top of the rivet head. Then you put two big bolts through the fire-hole door and a plate on the outside and then tighten them up so that the iron bar can't move. You can then get at the top of the rivet because it's only 1½ inches (3.8 cm) from the crown of the firebox. Four inches (10.2 cm) back there's four great pre-war Joe Whitworth nuts across that. So when you hold a normal caulking tool and tap it with the hammer it goes 'dooong' and your knuckles hit the nuts and all the skin is ripped off – it's really difficult to get at. Hence the piece of iron to enable you to squeeze off the edge of the hole on to the edge of the rivet. About ten minutes after I'd fixed up this creation there was no water and no leaks. However, the Scottish Boiler Insurance Company sent me a bill for £175 for supervision of the work so far! They seemed to be creating obstacles all the time – so I paid the bill and sacked them. Eventually, a man called John Gorley passed my boiler fit at inspection and he became a good friend of mine!

A steamroller can be a very dangerous piece of equipment. The rollers, of course, are smooth and in hilly country you don't have much grip. There have been a few famous steamroller disasters near where I live. One was in a place called Ramsbottom where every street seems to be steeply sloping; the local road roller ran away down a hill and straight through the gable end of a house at the bottom.

I have experienced similar catastrophe myself. During my steeple-jacking career, perhaps eighteen years ago, I got a job dismantling some beautiful Victorian chimney stacks. These were octagonal-shaped blocks of stone, about 18 inches (45.7 cm) across, with a 9-inch (22.8-cm) hole chopped through the middle. I couldn't bring myself to break them up with a hammer, throw them in a skip and send the invoice. So I borrowed a railer that weighed 3½ tons (and had no brakes) and I dragged it across Bolton one Sunday afternoon when there were no policemen about and parked it under a big tree in the grounds of a mansion I was working on. On Monday and Tuesday I constructed an aerial wireway, which was very similar to those that were used in Welsh slate quarries. By Thursday the stones were coming down the wire and old Donald was piling them up on the trailer. When we got one layer of rock all over this trailer, not knowing the pulling capabilities of a 1910 steamroller which has smooth steel wheels, we decided that we would take the engine and hook it on to the end of the trailer. We did this one Saturday afternoon and everything was lovely. We shoved the handle forward, opened the regulator and chuff chuff, we went down the road. The engine pulled so well that you couldn't tell the loaded trailer was on the back. We decided we would put two layers of stone on this trailer for the second journey. When it was loaded and you stood behind the trailer the chassis looked all bent and the tyres were pear-shaped underneath from the weight. I would say there was something in the region of 20 tons on this trailer. It was grossly overloaded for its size.

We hooked it on to the steamroller and set off. You could certainly tell there was something on the back now. When you came to a bit of a downer, the draw bar went bang bang on the back of the engine with a fearsome jolt and this had the effect of putting silver streaks on the rims of the wheels about 6 inches (15.2 cm) long. When it had stabilized it began to grip again. But it was very dodgy. This steamroller was nearly ready to become a sledge and not a vehicle!

While we were hauling the third and final trailer load, I had a 'phone call from a restaurant which is situated on top of a hill outside Bolton. The man at the other end said: 'I believe you've got these stones with holes in. We'd like some to put round our restaurant – to put plants in.' I said: 'Well how much will you give me?' And he said: '£80 for a wagon load.' I said: 'You're on, cock, delivered by steam power!' Then I thought: 'Good God! How are we going to get it up the hill?'

On the day we were due to deliver the load everything went wrong. It had rained all weekend, but we'd managed to get the engine back to my house with the trailer of rocks behind it. The grand plan was to attack the hill on Sunday. When I woke up on Sunday morning, the rain was still coming down. As I lit the fire I was full of apprehension and fear, but I thought that if the engine couldn't make it, at least we could chock up the trailer, unpin the engine and come home and then go back when the sun came out. It went up the first hill out of Bolton in the pouring rain, it didn't skid and there were no silver streaks on the wheels. There were a few undulations before we got to it and a right-hand bend called Hospital Brew, which is very steep. Steamrollers have two gears, slow and very slow, and I changed it into bottom gear, prayed to the good man upstairs, shoved the handle forward, opened the regulator and it was whaff, whaff, whaff, all the way up the hill. It burned all the paint off the funnel, but we got there. I was a happy man. Credit to Thomas Aveling who made this design in 1910.

In those days this restaurant wasn't quite as well off as it is now and behind the back of the car park, where the owner stored building materials, the ground was covered with a mixture of ballast and mud and rubbish in general. We were told to unload the stones into this compound and he gave us the £80. Really I wouldn't mind if drink could be blamed for what happened next, but it was in the days when the pubs shut at three o'clock, and they'd shut. When it was time to leave we came out of the car park in the far corner, then down a slip road that meets the main entrance road at an approximate angle of 45 degrees where – and I'll never forget the vision as long as I live – there's a cattle grid, a five-barred gate, a gas lamp, a flag pole and various half beer barrels full of shrubs. But there was this 45-degree bend at the bottom. Because we were in hilly country we'd got both pins in the wheels, we'd got the trailer, 3 hundredweight (152 kg) of coal, three stolen road lamps lit, and we'd got the £80. The grand plan was to arrive down on the level, have a pint here and a pint there and wind our way home in safety.

We were now coming down the hill towards the junction with the main road at the bottom. Weber, the young man who was steering, was only nineteen years old, but confident enough as he'd done quite a few miles with me. The man from the restaurant who had bought the stone from us, stood on the trailer to wave us off at the main gate. But steamrollers aren't designed for going down hills as steep as this. The braking system on them is next to useless, so we started going too fast. When the man from the restaurant heard the swearing, he decided he'd had enough. He jumped over the wall into the field and let me and Weber carry on at about 25, or 30 miles an hour (48 kmph), heading down the hill with a 45-degree bend at the bottom. There's no way with both pins in the back wheels and no differential gear (for us mechanically minded), we were ever going to get around the bend at the bottom. And I've omitted to mention that at the bottom of the hill there's a big stone pillar 2 feet (60 cm) thick, and 5 feet (1.5 m) wide with a 4-inch (10.2-cm) steam pipe down the middle. If we got past this big stone pillar and across the main entrance road, there was a big field. A steamroller entering a wet field at speed is like a bar of soap in a wet sink. It's course is completely unpredictable. This field was very narrow and at the edge of the field there was a 15-foot (4.6-m) drop into the back of a geriatric hospital. I had a terrible vision of a big hole in the side of this building, dead old ladies, twisted and bent National Health bedsteads and a huge bill at the end of the day. So I said to Weber: 'Aim for the pillar – at least it'll take a bit of steam out of it.'

We went fair and square on to the pillar front end. Bang! We hit the pillar and the top half of it took off towards heaven. I thought it would be racehorse mixture, ten of sand and one of cement, but it wasn't. They must have had an extra bag of cement when they built this pillar. The impact just chopped it off. The scraper on the front roller is ⅜-inch thick, 2 x 2½ inch (5 x 6 cm) angle iron and it was flattened into a straight plate as if it had been a 6- or 7-inch-wide (15- or 18-cm-wide) iron bar where it had hit the pillar. The top section of the pillar disappeared into the sky, complete with the steam pipe and the back side of a 'no entry' sign. It disintegrated and came showering down like shrapnel. The engine took off like Concorde – the front rose at least

Richard Trevithick's high pressure stationary engine, circa 1805. Trevithick was the first engineer to use steam at higher pressures; something Watt felt was too dangerous.

Top: Copper works in Cornwall at the height of the mining industry in the 1860s. There were over 650 beam engines working in the county in those years and things looked a lot different to the picturesque landscape we know today.
Above: The weaving shed at Queen Street Mill in Burnley. There were once over a thousand looms here powered by a tandem compound steam engine.
Opposite: A Cotton Mill in Preston, Lancashire in the 1920s.

Top: A portable steam engine made by Ransome and Sims.
Above: An Aveling and Porter steam-powered reaper, 1876. Early portable machines were not self-propelled, they had to be pulled by horses. At Rochester in Kent, Thomas Aveling built mobile traction engines and steam rollers.
Opposite top: A traction engine drawing a heavy load through the city streets impressed the locals in 1858.
Opposite below: One of Aveling's steam rollers at work in Hyde Park, London in 1866. The huge machine had a 12hp engine and its rollers were 3 feet (1 m) broad and 7 feet (2.2 m) in diameter.

Opposite top: An old photograph of an Aveling and Porter engine with wagons, circa 1890.
Opposite below: A Fowler 'Supreme Showman's steam traction engine', 1933. This type of engine was used to drive the rides at fairgrounds around the country.
Left and overleaf: Enthusiasts such as Len Crane in Wolverhampton are keeping the old machines and machinery alive by rebuilding and restoring them. This steam-powered crane was used by John Thompson's boiler makers to deliver their boilers to factories and to the docks for export.

12 feet (3.7 m) and the rear wheels came to rest momentarily on the top of the stump of the pillar.

It's amazing how on occasions like this you've time to think. And I thought: 'If only it was a traction engine instead of a roadroller.' A traction engine is made of wrought iron or steel at the front and the worst thing that could happen is you would dint the smoke box or break the front axle in two, and it's fairly easy to make a new one. But on a steamroller, the front half consists of about 3 tons of cast iron and you cannot drop 3 tons of cast iron from that elevation and expect it to stay in one piece. I didn't have long to wait. The front came crashing down. It dug a hole in the road 18 inches (45.7 cm) deep, the front forks broke into three pieces and the rollers carried on out the front. Another awful thought struck me: if the chains that did the steering had broken, the two rollers and what was left of the front forks would've gone away across the field and down through this hospital. It would have been like the Dambusters!

But the chains held, so the rollers were still out on the front. The engine had 200 lbs per square inch (14 kg per cm^2) in its belly and a raging fire and of course the boiler was at an angle of 45 degrees and stuck in the road. This is not the recommended angle for a locomotive boiler – in fact it's bad news. If there's no water where the fire is, it's going to blow the plug out, so you have to put the fire out pronto. I'd only brought the short shovel, so I had to stand on the axle boxes. The Tarmac was on fire and of course by this time a small crowd had gathered. And in the crowd there was a David Bailey with his camera and he was going round taking pictures of this terrible disaster. I was in a semi-state of shock – my brain had nearly clicked back in now, wondering where there was another pair of front forks.

I'd been round the front and looked at the damage. Another man who was standing in the background came over and said: 'My lad's got a breakdown wagon. Would you like me to give him a ring?' I said: 'Well, if you think it would lift the engine up I'd be very obliged to you.' He disappeared into the night. By now it was nearly dark. The David Bailey character carried on with his camera, taking pictures of the wreck, and then in a flash I remembered where there were two pairs of Aveling and Porter forks – leaning against a wall in a place called Dewsbury on the way to Leeds. To cut a long story short, I got the front forks for £75 and had it brought down the M62 on the back of a truck for £15, three telegraph poles and a pair of 2-ton chain blocks. By the following Wednesday the roller was back on its wheels again – a bit scarred and scratched with all the chains, but at least it was right. We'd had a run round the car park to prove that the crankshaft wasn't bent.

Every day during the course of this recovery operation a little lad had appeared with his newspaper bag on his back, a bit like me when as a youngster I used to go mithering steeplejacks and they didn't want to talk to me. I never spoke to him; I still wasn't completely recovered. Then on this final day, about Thursday, I was happy because everything was going well. He arrived with his paper bag and he said: 'Hey mister, you know that horse you had on the front? I've got its head, I've got its four legs and its tail.' But the torso part of the horse, which was the Aveling and Porter trademark, was still attached to the smokebox door. I said: 'Did you see this disaster, kid?' He replied: 'Oh yes, I only live over there in that house. I were having me tea with me mam and me dad and me dad said to me mam: "Bloody Hell! That's going fast for a steamroller." And then bang, crash, and all them cinders, and it were on fire, weren't it?' I asked him: 'Do you remember the man with the camera?' And he said: 'Oh yes, Mr Jones, him with the boat up his drive.' I said: 'Well, you go and see if I can borrow his negatives and I'll get the rest of this horse off the front of here for you.' Away he went and came back almost immediately. He said: 'Saturday morning he'll have the pictures.'

Saturday morning came and I was there at seven o'clock. The fire was lit, everything was going well. I thought, I'll not muck his eggs and bacon up; I'll give him a reasonable time. At nine o'clock, just a bit before our proposed departure time, I knocked on his front door. He came to the door looking a bit sheepish. He looked like there'd been a bereavement in the family. I said: 'I'm the man in the field with the traction engine.' He said: 'Aye. And I'm the silly bugger who forgot to take the lens cap off the camera!'

CHAPTER FIVE

RULING THE WAVES

The first half of the nineteenth century must have been a pretty bewildering time in which to live. Technological development was taking place at a fantastic rate and the economic and social changes that went with it were beginning to alter the whole structure of society. In 1820 it still wasn't possible to travel any faster than in Roman times. But within thirty years there was a network of railways over much of Britain, reducing journey times from days and weeks to a few hours. By the middle of the century railway travel had suddenly made the world seem a much smaller place. People could leave their villages for the first time and goods like coal and grain could be transported the length and breadth of the British Isles.

Then steam power was introduced to the oceans to make sea travel between the continents faster. Until this time ships had been propelled either by oars or great sails. The first steam-powered ships were propelled by paddle-wheels and were built in the early 1800s by men such as Patrick Bell in Scotland and an American, Robert Fulton, who experimented with steam-powered paddle-wheels, though the idea for the paddle-wheel as a means of propulsion for vessels dates back to ancient Egypt. The early paddle-steamers hadn't got a lot going for them; they were simply sailing ships with engines and paddle-wheels. They were built from wood, although angle irons for joining framework had been used from the earliest days of steam weren't very seaworthy and keeping them supplied with coal was problematic because the boilers were uneconomical. They were used mainly on rivers and very near the coastline. For the open sea, something better was needed.

The use of metal in the construction of fairly small boats began in the first half of the nineteenth century, but, for technical reasons, the general application of power to sea transport lagged about twenty years behind developments on land. Problems included getting a steam engine to propel a vessel through water. The first answer was to make the engine drive a pair of rotating paddles, one placed on either side of the vessel.

Almost as soon as the steam engine was invented there had been attempts to use it as a power to drive ships. Thomas Savery was a pioneer of the steam engine who built a 'contrivance with paddle-wheels to move becalmed ships'. He wanted the British Admiralty and Navy Board to use his designs, but met with no success. At around the same time, in the early 1700s, the Frenchman Denis Papin put a steam engine into a ship to use the steam to drive a paddle-wheel. But there was a design problem – how to translate the 'to and fro' motion of the piston into the circular motion needed for the paddle. Another problem was that the boilers couldn't produce enough pressure to provide suffi-cient power.

Jonathon Hulls, of Gloucestershire, patented his steam tow-boat in 1736, long before a successful rotative engine had been introduced. His experiments were made on the Avon at Evesham in 1737, the main idea being to have a Newcomen engine – the only sort then known – on a tow-boat in front of the vessel which it was intended to propel, con-nected by a tow-rope. Six paddles in the stern of the tow-boat were fastened to a cross axis connected by ropes to another axis which was turned by the engine. Hulls showed how to convert the motion of a piston rod into a rotatory motion, which is an essential principle in steam locomotion whether on land or water. He is described as 'Inventor of the Steam Boat' on a portrait at the Institute of Marine Engineers.

In the eighteenth century the idea of using steam propulsion for boats had been taken up in America and a number of American engi-neers came over to England to look at the engines of Newcomen and of Boulton and Watt to see how they might be able to use them for propelling boats. Most of their experiments involved the use of paddle-wheels, which were turned by steam engines. But there were other experiments where the boat was driven by what we now call hydraulic or jet propulsion – the engine drove a great pump, which forced a stream of water out from the stern of the boat, propelling it forwards.

The first turbine recorded was made by Hero of Alexandria 2000 years ago – it's probably obvious to most people that some power can be obtained from a jet of steam either by the reaction of the jet itself as in a rocket, or by its impact on some kind of paddle-wheel. The first widespread application of high-pressure steam engines was on steamboats and resulted in frequent explosions and disasters. Passengers were injured by flying fragments of boilers and engines, blown to pieces, scalded to death and blown off steamers to drown. Fatal accidents were also happening in factories and engineering works. This was all down to the poor quality of workmanship and materials used to manufacture the machinery, coupled with a lack of proper quality control.

Around this time a lot of people were involved in experiments with steam-powered vessels and there are many claims as to who actually invented the first working steamboat. In this country some people claim that William Symington was the true inventor of the steamship. He received financial support from Lord Dundas to build a steam-powered tug for use on his canal. In 1802 he built the *Charlotte Dundas*, which was used on the Forth-Clyde canal in Scotland. Named after the daughter of Lord Dundas, and described as the first practical steamboat, it had a Watt double-acting engine turning a crank on a paddle-wheel shaft. The boat was such a success that the proprietors of the canal were urged to adopt it as a new method of towing, but they declined for fear of danger to the banks. Lord Dundas then approached the Duke of Bridgewater, who gave Symington an order for eight boats. However, the Duke died without signing the contract and Symington had to give up in despair.

In America it is claimed that Robert Fulton invented the steamboat. He built a boat called the *Clermont*, which in 1807 moved slowly up the Hudson river against the current and without a sail. Her paddle-wheels creaked and splashed noisily; her crude steam engine shook the deck and black sooty smoke belched from the chimney, giving off sparks. *Clermont* went from New York to Albany on a 150-mile (241-km) trip, taking thirty-two hours at an average speed of 5 miles per hour (8 kmph). The boat was advertised to the public as the *North River Steamboat*. Fulton had carefully studied earlier inventions and put all of their best features together. The result was that he was able to build a steamboat that not only worked but was commercially successful as well. Not a single part of the *North River Steamboat* was his own invention, although he patented improvements on much of the machinery. His was the first useful steamboat, but it was the product of accumulated knowledge, not something that stood on its own as did those that preceded it. Fulton was the right man, in the right place, at the right time.

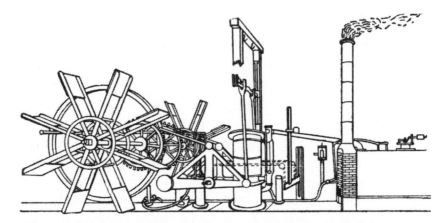

Above: The steam engine mounted in the *Clermont* and the ship's maiden voyage from New York to Albany in 1807.

In 1812 a Scottish engineer, Henry Bell, designed a small steamship called *Comet*, which he ran on the River Clyde. The first passenger vessel built in Europe, she was driven by a vertical single-cylinder engine of 3 horsepower (2.2 kw). She had paddle-wheels on each side and carried regular passengers between Glasgow, Greenock and Helensburgh. By 1814 five Scottish steamers were working regularly on British waters and by 1820 there were thirty-four. Within twenty years paddle-steamers were operating from most ports in Britain, and their number had reached 1,325. All these early steamships were quite small and were suitable only for use on inland or coastal waters; sailing ships still ruled the ocean waves.

The very first steamer to make a sea voyage was American. *Phoenix* steamed 13 miles (21 km) from Hoboken to Philadelphia. Very soon men on both sides of the Atlantic were dreaming of crossing the ocean by steam. The Americans won the race when the *Savannah* travelled from Georgia to St Petersburg, via Great Britain and the north European ports. She used twenty-five paddle-wheels and took twenty-nine days. It was a testing trip; all the coal had been consumed before the boat reached Ireland. It is said that they ended up burning the furniture and even the doors from the cabins to finish the Atlantic crossing. On the return trip the *Savannah* had to go under sail. From

Above: The *Comet* designed by Henry Bell was the first passenger steamship built in Europe, she ran on the River Clyde between 1812 and 1820.

Above: The *Rising Star*, first ocean-going British steamship.

Britain it was the *Rising Star*, built in London in 1821, that was the first to make the trip west. She had internal paddle-wheels and crossed from Gravesend to Valparaiso.

By the start of Queen Victoria's reign in the 1830s the paddle-steamer had proved its viability on shorter coastal routes, but the lucrative transatlantic trade was still dominated by American sailing packets. Then along came my hero, Isambard Kingdom Brunel. Brunel was an amazing man. If it had anything to do with engineering, he'd have a go at it. While he was building the Great Western Railway he began to develop the idea of linking the railway with a series of ships in a combined land and sea transport system. His dream was to link a steamship service to New York with the Great Western Railway at Bristol, so that you could buy a through ticket from Paddington to New York.

Brunel had decided right from the outset that his ships were going to be powered by steam. The SS *Great Britain*, which he built, was one of the outstanding engineering achievements of the Victorian age. It was the first big ocean-going vessel to be constructed from iron and driven by a steam-powered propeller and it revolutionized ocean travel. But when he first had the idea for this, people thought he was mad. Until then it had been thought that, although small steamships could be used on coastal routes, they were not practical for ocean crossings because they would need so much fuel that there would be no room left on board for any passengers or cargo. Brunel was a bit of a mathematician, though, and he worked out that while a ship's carrying capacity increases by the cube of its dimensions, its resistance, and hence the force needed to propel it increases by the square of its dimensions. As a result of this, he calculated, ships would need less energy per ton to propel them the larger they were.

The SS *Great Britain* wasn't Brunel's first steamship. In 1836, the year before Victoria came to the throne, he had persuaded the directors of the Great Western Railway to form the Great Western Steamship Company and had begun work on the SS *Great Western*, the first of three ships he built. The 1,320-ton paddle-steamer was launched in 1837 and it proved that a steamship could cross the Atlantic without running out of coal. On the oceans Britain led the way with steamers, drastically cutting down travel times. Sailing clippers took thirty-five days to travel to New York, and twenty-five days to return with a favourable wind. The SS *Great Western* sailed from Bristol to New York in fifteen days and fifteen hours. For speed, reliability and comfort it was a big improvement on the packets, but the ship had some serious weaknesses. Her sails had to be used in conjunction with her engines, and paddles did not perform well under ocean conditions. But the biggest drawback was the fact that the ship was built of wood and it was costly to construct wooden ships strong enough to withstand the stress from the engines.

Brunel knew that the SS *Great Western* represented the limit of what was possible with wood, which is why his next ship would have to be built from iron. But the size of iron ships was restricted by problems in using magnetic compasses. Fortunately, at this time a system of correcting magnets was devised by the Astronomer Royal, Professor Airey. The new system was installed on *Rainbow*, an iron paddle-steamer that visited Bristol in 1838. Two of Brunel's colleagues, Captain Christopher Claxton and William Patterson, reported favourably on the new system after joining *Rainbow* on a voyage to Antwerp. This made Brunel's mind up and he decided to go ahead with a new iron ship. To build it the Great Western Dock at Bristol was extended, warehouses and workshops were erected and construction machinery was installed. The SS *Great Western* was the largest vessel that had ever been built in the world up to this time, but Brunel knew it needed to be improved upon, so he turned his inventive mind to the problems of building an iron ship and of screw propulsion.

The initial plan for the new ship had been to incorporate into the design the largest-ever paddle-wheels, but he knew that paddles weren't really the best form of propulsion for crossing the ocean. Paddle-wheels are large and complicated in comparison with the modern propeller, and their depth in the water can affect their performance. When a paddle-steamer is heavily loaded, the wheels sink further below the surface. In rough seas, when a paddle-steamer rolls, one wheel may come out of the water while the other is completely submerged. Before the 1860s marine engines consumed so much fuel that by the time a ship was loaded with cargo there was only space left for coal for a few days' steaming without stopping to refuel. Far-sighted people in the shipping business could see what needed to be done to make a steamship that would be commercially profitable in competition with sailing ships. First, it would have to have a much more efficient and economical engine than anything that had been developed up to this time. Second, metal construction was essential to take the stresses and strains of power propulsion. And finally, the ship would have to be bigger in order to be more economical to run per ton-mile and therefore more profitable. To make any of these changes there needed to be something better than the paddle as a means of propulsion and by the 1840s a new propeller, attached to the stern of the ship below the water line, was being perfected. The screw propeller was the answer.

The development of the screw propeller was one of the most important in the whole history of seafaring. In Britain it began in 1836 when Francis Pettit Smith, who was a farmer by profession, took out a patent placing the screw between the sternpost and the rudder. A promotional organization was formed called the Screw Propeller Company. They built a ship called *Archimedes*, which was launched in 1838. Brunel had been watching these developments with great interest; the keel of his new ship was laid on 1 July 1839. Ten months later *Archimedes* arrived in Bristol and demonstrated her revolutionary propeller. Brunel chartered her for six months and this convinced him that the propeller system represented a huge advance on the paddle-wheel and he needed to make changes to his design. The engine that had been originally planned couldn't be adapted, so a design based on the 'Triangle' engine patented by his father, Sir Marc Brunel, was substituted. The ship's name was SS *Great Britain* and Brunel, Claxton and the consulting engineer, Thomas Guppy, formed a building committee.

One of the things that had made possible the construction of a large ocean-going, steam-powered, iron-hulled ship were the advances that steam had brought about in the iron and steel industries. The most significant of these advances happened in 1839 in Patricroft, near Manchester, where James Naysmyth perfected the steam-hammer. Until then the capacity of the old water-powered hammers limited the forging of large pieces of steel. History has it that when Brunel was planning to build SS *Great Britain* as a paddle-ship, one of the great problems he was faced with in building paddles for a ship of this size was finding somebody who had a big enough hammer to construct a crankshaft that would go across the whole width of the ship. The problem was solved when Naysmyth developed the steam-hammer, and it is said that he did so for the SS *Great Britain*, but then Brunel changed his mind and decided on the screw or propeller rather than the paddles. So Naysmyth was left with this steam-hammer, but it wasn't a failure, because it enabled the iron industry to make bigger ingots to be put through the rollers to make bigger plates for building bigger ships – and bigger everything.

Naysmyth improved his steam-hammer in 1843 so that steam was able to push the hammer down with tremendous force as well as lift it up. The steam-hammer made possible the forging of iron beams and steel plates larger than any that had ever been produced before. But it could also be controlled to make it descend so lightly that it could crack an eggshell without smashing the egg. When Naysmyth demonstrated it in 1845 he was loudly cheered by a group of spectators because such a saving in time in the performance of similar work by steam, as opposed to manual labour, had never been witnessed.

The great advances in the development of iron and iron angles and plates as a result of the progress that had been made in the iron and steel industries were yet another factor that persuaded Brunel to build the SS *Great Britain* in iron. The ship's hull is clinker built – constructed of wrought-iron plates, which were shaped and riveted in the dock where she was built. They measure about 6 x 2½ feet (1.8 x 0.8 m), overlap horizontally and are connected by two rows of rivets. This overlap gave 15 per cent more strength than if they had been laid edge to edge, and the hull has always been remarkably watertight.

Wrought iron is a malleable, workable metal that is strong under tension and highly rust-resistant. It is made from cast iron in a process called puddling. Two further stages involving reheating and rerolling are needed before the finished iron bar is ready. It is the oldest commercial form of iron and was used extensively in the nineteenth century. As well as being used for the SS *Great Britain* it was employed for Robert Stephenson's Conwy and Britannia tubular bridges, for anchors and for anything requiring its high-tensile strength. In mid-nineteenth-century Britain about 3 million tons were produced every year.

The SS *Great Britain*, launched on 19 July 1843, was a landmark in the progress of steamship development. She was named and launched by the Prince Consort, who travelled from Paddington to Bristol in a special train, accompanied by Brunel and Daniel Gooch, his locomotive engineer. This massive vessel was 322 feet long (98 m), and of 3,675 tons displacement, and nothing like her had ever been seen before. She was the world's first fully-powered big steamship, carrying masts, spars and sails to help her engines, but the engines were there to drive her all the time.

The SS *Great Britain* had to be hauled back into her dock for the installation of her engines and was not ready for sea trials until late in the following year. Because the locks of the Cumberland basin had not been widened as the Bristol Dock Company had agreed, she stuck fast. Brunel released the ship from the floating harbour by partially dismantling the locks at night. It was this difficulty they had in getting the ship out of the port that signalled the decline of Bristol as a great maritime centre and the end of Brunel's dream of the direct Paddington-New York link. The SS *Great Western* had already been transferred to the more convenient port of Liverpool in 1843 and it was decided to base the SS *Great Britain* there as well. The ship still had to overcome fears about her safety and so, on 26 July, she sailed for New York with just fifty passengers and 600 tons of cargo. She crossed the Atlantic in fourteen days twenty-one hours in grand style, and they didn't have to resort to burning any doors or furniture. In fact, there was a bit of coal left when she reached her destination, to the credit of Mr Brunel. Of course the ship received a tremendous welcome as she steamed up the Hudson and into the port of New York.

The SS *Great Britain* had a long and interesting career. She was re-engined at a fairly early stage in her life. She did the Atlantic crossings, she took convicts to Australia, and eventually the engines were removed and she was turned into a sailing ship for the remainder of her days. She came to a sad end near the Falkland Islands with a big hole cut in her side as a coal station for the illustrious British Navy. Finally one day it was decided that her useful life as a coal bunker was over, so they took her out to sea and scuttled her. However, she didn't sink right down to the bottom and she languished there for many years. Much later some bright spark somewhere in England decided what a famous ship she was and came up with the idea that she should be rescued. They sent a Dutchman with a great barge to the Falkland Islands to get her out of the sand and bring her all the way back to Bristol, where she now lies in the very dock in which she was built.

The importance of the ship lay in the prestige she conferred on Brunel, who was retained as the consultant engineer for the Navy's pioneer screw steam warship. He was also able to embark on an even more ambitious ship-building project for the commercial market. The SS *Great Britain* is now regarded as a landmark in ship design, but she was never really a commercial success and eventually bankrupted the

Above: Brunel's SS *Great Britain*, first steamship (and first iron-built ship) to cross the Atlantic in 1845.

company that built her. A perusal of Brunel's papers and correspondence held at Bristol University shows that commercial failures like the SS *Great Britain* meant that her designer wasn't always popular with shareholders. And he wasn't liked any better by many of the contractors who worked for him. Because he was a perfectionist who liked to check on every detail of his projects and change the specification if he thought of a better way of doing things, he was very difficult to work with. This can be seen very clearly in his final great project and his partnership on it with the eminent ship-builder John Scott Russell.

In 1851 Brunel began designs for a ship four times the size of the SS *Great Britain*. His plans were for a vessel that would be capable of taking a year's exports to India in one trip and returning without refuelling. This was the SS *Great Eastern*, which Brunel designed with a double iron hull split into twenty-two compartments. This great monster of the oceans, very appropriately called Leviathan to start with, was 700 feet (213 m) long and had three sources of propulsion: two paddle-wheels each 58 feet (18 m) across and a single screw propeller that was 24 feet (7.3 m) across, which would be driven by a separate engine. To save fuel when possible, the ship was built with six masts, giving it 58,500 square feet (5,435 m²) of sail. The SS *Great Eastern* would be the queen of all ships. But its building cast a shadow over Brunel's last years. There was little doubt that a ship of such size would be pushing the boundaries of existing technology, and it was more than half a century before anybody attempted to build anything as big again.

Brunel was appointed engineer for the project. John Scott Russell, one of the leading marine architects of the day, was commissioned to build the hull. Scott Russell was primarily an engineer and naval architect rather than a mathematician, but his name is well known to applied mathematicians today through his discovery of the solitary wave. Born in Glasgow in 1808 where his father was a parish schoolteacher, Scott Russell graduated from Glasgow University at the age of seventeen and moved to Edinburgh, where he taught maths at an academy that may have been founded by himself and a friend. In the 1830s he developed a prototype passenger-carrying steam carriage, but it met with opposition from the road trustees and the venture failed. He had more success with the Union Canal Company, investigating the feasibility of steam-powered canal transport and studying the connection between resistance to motion and wave generation. Scott Russell worked for a ship-builder in Greenock and then moved to London in 1844 with his wife and two young children. He worked on a railway magazine and became secretary of the Society of Arts, a post that led to major involvement in planning the Great Exhibition of 1851. He was increasingly involved in the design of yachts, boats, barges and ships and became director of a ship-building company.

Scott Russell had his tender accepted to build and fit out the SS *Great Eastern* as well as provide the paddle engines and boilers for £275,200. His price was hopelessly optimistic. Brunel had originally estimated £500,000 and it's hard to understand how such an experienced ship-builder thought it could be done so cheaply. As it turned out, it couldn't, and Brunel soon fell out with him. It took a lot longer to build the ship than had originally been anticipated, they were always running out of money and Scott Russell was always at loggerheads with Brunel over financial matters.

The building of the ship was also dogged by minor setbacks, which seemed insoluble at the time. There were problems with construction because of the size of the project and Brunel's relationship with Scott Russell, which in turn had a good deal to do with the contractual arrangements. Brunel had maintained overall control of the project, despite the fact that Scott Russell was ultimately responsible for building it. Brunel's attention to detail and his insistence on making alterations to the plans slowed everything down, caused the costs to escalate and made things impossible for Scott Russell.

Brunel's relationships with contractors, shareholders and business partners wasn't helped by the fact that he always had so many projects on the go at the same time. While the SS *Great Eastern* was being built in London on the Isle of Dogs, he was also busy extending his broad-gauge railway empire from Devon into Cornwall. This included building the Royal Albert Bridge, which carries the line over the River Tamar at Saltash. The SS *Great Eastern* bankrupted Scott Russell and Brunel took over the construction himself. It was six months before he managed to get the ship into the water and all the difficulties he'd had with her construction, added to the problems of trying to get her launched, exhausted even the prodigious energies of Brunel. The huge and costly effort of launching the SS *Great Eastern* sideways into the Thames in January 1858, and preparing it for its first sea trials the following September, proved to be too much for him. The day before the sea trials there was an explosion. Somebody had forgotten to undo a stopcock on a feed water heater and the pressure built up and blew the back funnel off. The news of this setback on top of all the strain he was under was the final blow for Brunel and he collapsed on deck. He'd suffered a stroke, from which he died on 15 September 1859. His great friend Robert Stephenson, who remained a staunch supporter throughout all his troubles with the SS *Great Eastern*, died within a few weeks of him. Right at the end this massive project was too much of a disappointment for Brunel. In the last known photograph of him, taken on the deck of the enormous ship, this is visible in his face. It's a very sad picture – he's not even got his tall shiner on and his cigar's not going. He looks about seventy and yet he was only fifty-two years old at the time. He died shortly after the photograph was taken.

The SS *Great Eastern* was jinxed from the start and never made any money. It had sailings to Australia and at the end of its life was turned into a cable-laying ship and laid the first cable across the Atlantic.

Above: The launch of Brunel's giant SS *Great Eastern* steamship.

There are some beautiful etchings of it with these great drums of cable inside. Then it went to Liverpool as a floating advertising vessel and finally to Glasgow. The sad fate of the SS *Great Eastern* came to an end in November 1888 when the ship was sold piecemeal at auction. The firm of Henry Bath and Sons bought the hull for breaking up and had great trouble demolishing it – it had been made so well and so much magnificent engineering had gone in to its construction. They had no cutting gear and no oxyacetylene burners, so all the rivets had to have their heads knocked off and be punched out of the plate. Quite often in scrapyards you see pieces of plate with rivet holes all round the edge and I often wonder where they've come from – some tank or possibly the side of a ship.

Despite the public acclaim Brunel received for much of his work, he also came in for a lot of criticism. The building of the ship was furiously attacked by the press, who accused Brunel of megalomania. You can see, particularly in the criticisms of his design for the ship and his attempts to launch it, that his genius wasn't always recognized in its time. Yet today the SS *Great Eastern* is regarded as the prototype of modern luxury liners. Brunel embodied some of the best values of his age, particularly hard work and innovation. The skill of making things were highly valued; there was little sympathy for weakness and none at all for idleness, and above all there was an unbending faith in the ability to get things done, however great the challenge. It seems to me that these are all values that we've lost and if we still had them today, perhaps Britain would still be a major industrial power.

Brunel had been able to move between the marine, civil, railway and mechanical engineering fields, which later engineers were not able to do as projects grew bigger and the profession began to divide into more specialist fields. He was a great individualist – a quality that was greatly admired by the Victorians. He had tremendous vision and energy, but he liked to be able to do everything himself. He wasn't really a good team player. One of the main reasons for the problems with the SS *Great Eastern* was Brunel's insistence on being in charge of every detail of the building rather than letting Scott Russell get on with his part of it. Scott Russell gets rather a bad press from the Brunel supporters, but, having seen some of his wonderful designs for the Royal

Navy, I think they could be wrong. The greatest of these designs was HMS *Warrior*, the first ocean-going iron-hulled battleship in the world.

During 1858 and 1859, while the SS *Great Eastern* was awaiting completion, Scott Russell had started to try and re-establish himself as a ship-builder. As well as building some ships himself, he consulted with the Admiralty over the design of the HMS *Warrior* – a ship that was planned to be the largest, fastest and most powerful battleship of its time. The Navy was a very conservative institution and, at first, it had been reluctant to commission any of these new iron steamships. At the end of the Napoleonic War in 1815 the most powerful ships in the world were wooden. Iron had already been used in British ship-building, with iron barges in use before the end of the eighteenth century. The first armed iron ship was the *Nemesis*, a paddle gunboat owned by the Honourable East India Company. She was built in 1839 and used in the Opium War of 1841. Large paddle-frigates were also built, such as HMS *Terrible*. This was launched in 1845 and fought during the Crimean War, but with only nineteen guns she was very vulnerable. The screw propeller was first used effectively on a military vessel in 1852, when the French *Le Napoleon* started a brief arms race. Britain's first steam-powered warship, HMS *Agamemnon* was launched soon after in reply.

With the advances in iron ship-building and the introduction of practical steam-propelled warships, the development of iron warships was inevitable. In April 1845 the Admiralty set up a tug-of-war between the paddle-steamer *Alecto* and the propeller-driven *Rattler*. *Rattler* won the competition, dragging the *Alecto* behind her at a speed of 2.8 knots (1.9 kmph). This brought the dominance of the paddle-wheel to an end and the stage was set for the development of HMS *Warrior*. The background to Scott Russell's association with HMS *Warrior* began as far back as 1851, which is when he first thought about an iron-hulled and armoured steam warship. Three years later, events in the Crimean War, drew attention to the subject when the wooden ships of the time proved to be an unequal match for the latest developments in shellfire. So Scott Russell produced designs for a ship with an outer skin of thick iron armour plate backed by wood and submitted them to the Admiralty.

Nothing happened for three years, but by the end of the 1850s relations with France had deteriorated. In 1858 a new French fleet was commissioned. The first ship was *La Gloire*, a wood-framed frigate clad in iron and the most advanced warship of its day. The Admiralty's response to restore Britain's naval prestige was bold – the building of the world's first iron-hulled battleship. For this Scott Russell was asked to prepare a larger version of his design. At the same time the Navy's chief constructor, Isaac Watts, prepared his own design, which was very similar. HMS *Warrior* is in fact a combination of Scott Russell's and Watt's designs. But in spite of his contribution to its design, Scott Russell's bid for the contract to build the ship was rejected on account of price and time and it was given to the Thames Ironworks at Blackwall. Regardless of this, HMS *Warrior* was regarded as very much a Scott Russell ship. Because of all his pioneering work on the development of iron warships and the fact that HMS *Warrior* was based so much on the designs he submitted to the Admiralty, it is as much his ship as anybody's.

The ship is a great example of Victorian inventiveness and ingenuity. Its features include retracting funnels; a propeller that could be lifted out of the water; sail and steam for maximum speed; an iron fortress construction; and pumps to move fresh water around the ship. Many of these features, like the combination of sail and speed and the actual shape of the boat, were to be found in the design for the SS *Great Eastern* and it's hard to know which of them were Brunel's and which Scott Russell's. Warrior only took a year to build and it didn't have any of the problems of the SS *Great Eastern*. So perhaps the accounts that place all of the blame for Brunel's problems on Scott Russell are doing him an injustice.

The launch of HMS *Warrior* in 1860 marked the beginning of a new era of engineering with three factors coming together. First, it saw the end of the heroic age of engineering when an individual like Brunel could tackle anything and the beginning of an age of specialization in engineering. Second, it witnessed the rise of the entrepreneurial engineer and the big engineering companies. And, finally, it saw the application to warfare of the technology of the Industrial Revolution. The man who manufactured the guns on HMS *Warrior* embodied all of these changes. He was the great inventor, engineer and gun-maker William Armstrong, who dominated the world of engineering in the second half of Victoria's reign as he built up the mighty industrial giant of W. G. Armstrong and Company. Armstrong was one of the many engineering associates of Brunel who befriended his family when he died and he took Brunel's son, Henry, into his works at Elswick as an apprentice. It was here that Armstrong carried on what Brunel had started with his iron ships, by building iron warships.

When Victoria came to the throne in 1837 he was practising as a lawyer in Newcastle but he was spending his spare time pursuing his passion for all things mechanical and scientific. Along with Henry Watson, Armstrong designed his first hydraulic engine for Robert Stephenson's High Level Bridge at Newcastle. Unfortunately it produced only 5 horsepower (3.7 kw) and was not a success. In 1846 he successfully converted one of the cranes at Newcastle docks to hydraulic power by modifying the rotary principle into a one-stroke piston and adapting the design into that of a crane. By 1847 Armstrong was no longer practising in law and he had set up the Newcastle Cranage Company (W. G. Armstrong and Company) with four associates. He opened his Elswick works on the banks of the Tyne to manufacture hydraulic cranes and all manner of engineering equipment and machinery like lathes, pumps, winding engines, steam engines and dock gates.

It was the Crimean War that prompted Armstrong to produce his revolutionary new system of artillery. Up until this time cannon had been muzzle-loading and they had fired round projectiles – the traditional cannon. Armstrong designed the breech-loading gun, which fired shells. By 1858 the Armstrong cannon had become the standard field artillery for the British Army. He gave up his patents to the government and in return was granted a knighthood, appointed Chief Engineer of Rifled Ordnance and later Superintendent of the Royal Gun Factory at Woolwich. Between 1859 and 1863 Elswick was the monopoly supplier of heavy arms to the British government. By February of 1863, however, Armstrong was forced to resign from his government position. The government announced that, because of high costs, it was to terminate all its gunnery contracts with Elswick. In order to survive, Armstrong dropped his patriotic inclinations and was very successful selling arms to both sides in the American Civil War. During the 1860s the demand for Elswick cannons became worldwide.

By this time Armstrong's output had been extended to bridge-building. Among his projects was Newcastle's Swing Bridge, which is still operating today. With the building of the Swing Bridge, Elswick was opened up to big ships and Armstrong was able to add ship-building to his ever-expanding empire. W. G. Armstrong and Company was now a leading player in the armaments game, able to design, build, equip and arm, from blast furnace to battleship. In 1867 the company began to build iron warships and over the next fifteen years twenty ships were built. For the last fifteen years of the century Armstrong's company led the world in the manufacture of iron war-ships and armaments. By the 1890s the manufacture of arms and warships had become one of Britain's biggest industries. Armstrong, the innovator and inventor, had turned a brilliantly successful engi-neering firm into a symbol of imperial might. His Elswick and Scotswood factories employed 30,000 men. Business was booming. As well as providing ships for the Royal Navy, Elswick built for the navies of fifteen other countries at this time. The Japanese Navy was one of Armstrong's biggest customers, and by the time of the Russo-Japanese War at the beginning of the next century Elswick-built ships made up almost half of the Japanese fleet. Most of the Russian fleet had been built further down the Tyne at Hawthorn Leslie's and Swan Hunter's yards, so the rivalry in Newcastle's pubs between the workers from the two yards, as the ships they'd built blew each other out of the water, must have been interesting.

The development of ironclad steamships was only possible because of the iron and steel industry's ability to meet demands. Bigger and more fuel-efficient furnaces produced cheap iron. The ship-building industry is the perfect illustration of the great progress that had been made in iron and steel production and engineering as bigger and faster ships were built to cross the oceans. Some of the most famous sailed under the flag of the Cunard Line. Samuel Cunard was born in Canada in 1787. He established the British and North American Royal Mail Steam Packet Company, later known as the Cunard Line, in 1839 with four ships. One of these was the *Britannia* and Cunard himself was at the helm as she sailed from Liverpool to Boston. Her fourteen-day-eight-hour voyage marked the beginning of regular transatlantic service by steamship. She was met by crowds and a great fanfare in Boston, and on one occasion when she was caught in ice in the harbour, people came out with pick axes and shovels to clear a path for the *Britannia* to sail. She marked the appearance of what was to become the famous orange-red funnels with a black top and small black bands. In 1842 Charles Dickens sailed on the *Britannia* to America and described how he hated the voyage. He said his cabin was cramped and small and he feared for his life when he saw sparks flying towards the sails from the funnel. At the time, people still trusted sails more than steam.

The development of the ironclad steamship transformed the geographical nature of the ship-building industry. The wooden ship-building industry was located in the south and south-west of Britain, but was soon replaced by the new iron-steamship yards of the northern industrial regions, particularly on the Tyne at Newcastle and on the Clyde around Glasgow. By the middle of the nineteenth century more efficient steam engines, in particular the compound engine developed by John Elder in 1854, made ships more efficient. Less coal was needed, leaving more space for cargo.

John Elder was one of the great men of steam engines to come out of the ship-building and engineering works of the Clyde. He was born in Glasgow in 1824, the son of the famous marine engineer David Elder. After an education at the city's high school and a brief period of study at the university, he gained an engineering apprenticeship with Robert Napier, where he took charge of the drawing office. He made good progress and by 1852 became a partner in Randolph, Elder and Company, and in 1860 took over the Govan Old Shipyard. In 1863 the firm moved to Fairfield Shipyard, where they employed 4,000 men in ship-building and engineering. Elder is most renowned for his contribution to marine engineering, in particular the development of the marine compound engine from the 1850s onwards. This engine consumed much less coal than any other engine at the time. As the design progressed, power was increased and the fuel consumption and friction in the engine reduced even further, thus the marine engine was made much more economical and powerful. Elder's exploration of triple and quadruple expansion engines affected the design of marine engines long after his death in 1869.

Within twenty-five years of the launch of SS *Great Britain*, massive advances had been made in the building of propeller-driven iron steamships. The *Russia* was Cunard Line's first entirely propeller-driven ship. She was launched in 1867 and easily won the Blue Riband competition with her new technology, crossing the Atlantic in eight days. She could reach a speed of 14 knots (26 kmph). Some of the most highly developed reciprocating steam engines were built for steamships in the second half of the nineteenth century. They were compact, powerful and economical on fuel. The steam was expanded in three stages, in high-, intermediate- and low-pressure cylinders. This system was introduced for marine use in 1871, the object being to use the steam as economically as possible, which is best achieved when the steam is expanded in a number of small stages. The Clyde had been the birthplace of the steamship – the *Charlotte Dundas* – and the river continued to play a major role in the development of the steamship with liners, battleships, cruisers and tugs, all built in the dozens of yards that sprang up along the banks of the river. At the turn of the century, 50 per cent of the world's ships were built on the Clyde.

By the end of the nineteenth century new forms of power were being introduced with gas, electricity and hydraulic power being used to do many of the things that steam engines had done. Armstrong was at the forefront of many of these developments because, as well as his

Above: The *Russia*, Cunard's first entirely propeller-driven ship, launched in 1867.

entrepreneurial ability and capacity for hard work, he had those other great qualities that were so much admired by the Victorians – desire for innovation and inventiveness to match. His innovations are best seen today in the house that he built, Cragside in Northumberland. The first house in the world to be lit by electricity, it became known as the 'palace of a modern magician' because of all of the examples of Armstrong's ingenuity in the field of hydraulics and engineering scattered around it and its grounds.

Armstrong's first concept of hydraulic power occurred to him when he was fishing. While he was watching the idle turn of a waterwheel he realized that the latent energy could be used more effectively if the flow was regular and concentrated in just one column. As for electricity, as early as 1840 he had learned about an engineer who received an electrical discharge from an emission of high-pressure steam and it was from this that the principle of hydroelectric energy was derived. He wrote papers and gave lectures on the subject and then, while he was still practising as a solicitor, he was made a fellow of the Royal Society. Armstrong was perhaps the greatest innovator of the Victorian age and nothing he attempted was a failure. But he didn't seem to have quite the same bravado as Brunel. That was to be found in a man who served his engineering apprenticeship with Armstrong.

Charles Parsons was one of the greatest engineers that this country has produced. He was the man who really invented the first successful steam turbine, which revolutionized electricity generation and marine transport and ensured that steam would continue to be used in the age of electricity. The youngest son of the Third Earl and Countess of Ross, Parsons was born in London in 1854 and brought up in Ireland, where he received his early education at home. From a young age he showed an interest in mechanics and engineering, and attended university at Trinity College, Dublin, and later at Cambridge.

The modern steam turbine as perfected by Parsons is a development of the windmill in some ways. Basically, jets of steam turn the blades of a rotor. The steam expands as it leaves the guide blades and makes the thing go round, just like the wind turning a windmill. But a turbine is enclosed, so it can achieve much greater pressures. Even as far back as Watt's era great interest had been shown in the development of the turbine. But Watt was as sceptical about it as he was about the development of high-pressure steam. In Britain there were no less than 200 patents taken out for gas and steam turbines between 1784 and 1884, which was the year Parsons patented his design for a steam turbine – the first successful one. Before this, progress had been very slow in the field of turbines. They were very inefficient, wasting a lot of energy from the steam and revving too fast. Of course, with the centrifugal forces created, some of them blew to pieces, sending debris flying at half the speed of a rifle bullet. It wasn't until Charles Parsons made his turbine that they really got to grips with the design.

Parsons realized that the problem with most of the early turbines was the fact that the steam expanded in one go, creating too much speed and inefficiency. He decided that he would use a series of blades to let the steam come in at a very high pressure and then expand as the blades got bigger. This made the turbine more economical and is basically how a modern turbine works. In his own words Parsons 'dealt with the turbine problem in a very different way'. He knew that if the turbine was to be accepted, the speed needed to be moderated. His design had fifteen stages of expansion – in other words, there were fifteen sets of blades. Of course this had the effect of slowing down the velocity of the steam. This type of moderate-speed turbine was much more economical and is called compounding. It was a brilliant innovation that enabled the turbine to be put to much more of a practical use.

In 1888 Parsons installed his first successful turbine in the Forth Banks power station in Newcastle upon Tyne. It was the first public power station to be powered by a steam turbine. In the following year he set up his own manufacturing plant at Heaton Works near Newcastle. Three 4-ton 100-kilowatt steam generators were installed in Cambridge Power Station in 1895 and provided the first electric street lighting in the town. Turbines were much cheaper to build than the more cumbersome reciprocating steam engines and they easily reached the speeds needed for generating electric power. The cheap electricity transformed people's lives. From the 1880s street lighting was becoming universal in cities and major towns. This led to a cut in crime and it also meant that people could work through the night.

It brought along with it electric trains and electric tramcars and all manner of electrically driven apparatus – even early vacuum cleaners by the 1900s. Trams and trains enabled the populations of big cities to move out into what we refer to now as suburbia. They could then easily travel into the city to work, and could enjoy escaping to the countryside or the seaside at weekends.

Parsons soon realized that the steam turbine could also be used for many other things. One of the major uses was to power ships, and in 1894, with a group of five friends, he formed the Marine Steam Turbine Company and started producing steam turbines for this purpose. The first turbines were regarded more as toys than as a major invention, but by1892 Parsons had developed his turbine from being about 4 kilowatts to about 100 kilowatts. By 1895 he was aware that there was enough power here to drive small boats, so he decided that he would build one and show the world what the steam turbine in marine form was capable of doing.

The story of *Turbinia* is one of the truly great engineering tales. In 1897, as part of her Diamond Jubilee, Queen Victoria was reviewing her great naval fleet at Spithead on the Solent. It was the largest collection of warships ever to have been gathered together at anchorage, with five columns of ships 6 miles (10 km) long including fifty battleships. This was when Britain ruled the waves and the crowned heads of Europe were all at Spithead to marvel at the power and the might of the British fleet. Then in the midst of it all along came an uninvited guest – Mr Parsons in his *Turbinia*. The little 44-ton experimental steam-turbine vessel could actually do 34 knots (63 kmph), an incredible speed for anything travelling on water at the time. Nobody had seen a ship go that fast anywhere in the world before. It sped past all the conventional vessels at Spithead and couldn't be stopped. The fastest destroyers of the day could do only 27 knots (50 kmph). The bold crew consisted of the director of Parsons's Marine Steam Turbine Company, Alan Campbell-Swinton, with Charles Parsons FRS as chief engineer and Dr Gerald Stoney FRS stoking up the boilers in the engine rooms.

Parsons's revolutionary vessel astonished the world. With it he made his point, not only to the Admiralty but also to all the foreign naval representatives present, that his boat *Turbinia* was faster by far than any other vessel. It was this sort of confidence and bravado that typified the engineers of the Victorian age and helped them to capture the public imagination and become contemporary heroes.

The success of *Turbinia* really amounted to two innovations: the steam turbine for ship propulsion and the slenderness of the hull. The steam turbine could no longer be ignored and the Royal Navy soon realized that it was the thing of the future. Soon after his exploits at Spithead, Parsons spent a great deal of time manufacturing turbine-powered warships. The turbine was soon adopted for all new Navy ships as well as for great ocean-going liners. But poor *Turbinia* had a rather unfortunate fate. Parsons sailed across the Channel to Paris with her after his display at Spithead. She was not much more than a canal boat, with a beam of only 8 or 9 feet (2.4 or 2.7 m) and about 60 feet (18.2 m) long. Returning to the Tyne, they parked her up and continued building turbines in the turbine works. Across the river, Robert Stephenson and Company had a boat-building yard and when they launched one of their boats it came straight across the river and chopped the little *Turbinia* in half. There are famous pictures of her on the quayside all bent in two – a sad end to such a famous and pioneering ship. However, she was patched up eventually and put on display in the Discovery Museum in Newcastle upon Tyne, where she can be seen today.

It is said that Charles Parsons sketched the original drawing for the reaction blades in his turbine on the back of an envelope. It was so successful it took £100,000 of research to improve it by only 2 per cent, which in my opinion is testimony to the instinctive knowledge and genius of Mr Parsons. Within ten years of the launch of *Turbinia* several turbine vessels were in service crossing the Atlantic. The steam turbine had almost replaced the reciprocating steam engine on the oceans. Nearly all of the major ocean-going liners on the Atlantic run, such as the *Queen Mary*, launched in 1934, *Queen Elizabeth* (1938) and the *United States* (1951), were propelled by steam turbines. Immediately after his exploits at Spithead, Parsons's first orders came from the Navy.

In 1898 the Royal Navy placed an order with him for a turbine-driven destroyer, HMS *Viper*. Up to this time Parsons had invested £24,000 in the development of the marine steam turbine, but it was now paying off. The Navy was so pleased with HMS *Viper* that they ordered another turbine destroyer, which they called HMS *Cobra*. Both boats easily passed their sea trials and almost matched *Turbinia*'s speed. But In 1901 disaster struck. HMS *Viper* went on the rocks off the Channel Islands and broke in two. No lives were lost, but *Cobra*'s was a different story. Seventy-seven men drowned when the ship just broke in two on its delivery voyage from the Tyne. The stresses and strains of the turbine were probably too much for the slender construction of the hull. There were a lot of men who worked for Charles Parsons on board the ship on that maiden voyage, and he never really got over the fact that some of his own men were drowned. But the Admiralty didn't lose confidence in Parsons and it ordered many more Navy vessels that would be driven by steam turbines.

The *King Edward* was built in 1901, the first commercial steam-turbine-driven ship in the world and therefore on a par with Brunel's SS *Great Britain*. It was built on the Clyde for a consortium including the ship-builder William Denny of Dumbarton, Charles Parsons, and John Williamson, who operated the ship. But there was one main problem with using the turbine in marine propulsion. It was a phenomenon called cavitation and occurred when the screw was rotated above certain limits, causing a great loss of power. The solution was to ensure a large surface area in the water by having very wide blades. Another problem with the turbine was that it was initially suitable only for speeds over 16 knots (29.6 kmph). In order to adapt it to slower vessels a system called the combination system was introduced. This involved a reciprocating engine taking the first part of the expansion of steam, and the turbine taking the last part. The reciprocating engine expands the steam to around atmospheric pressure and the turbine continues to expand the steam until it is down to the pressure in the condenser. The large, fast turbines could deal with the high-pressure portion of the expansion as well as a reciprocating machine, which is why the turbine was successful in the faster ships.

The next step was to test geared turbines in bigger boats. In 1909 Charles Parsons refitted the cargo steamer *Vespasian* with geared turbine engines and it was a success. The new machinery was 15 per cent more efficient than the reciprocating engine, and an alteration to the propeller increased this to 22 per cent. The new machinery, which was much lighter than the old, had a high- and a low-pressure turbine, each driving a pinion at 1,400 revolutions, gearing into a spur wheel on the screw making seventy revolutions per minute. Gearing promised to play a very important part in war vessels by being more economical at low speeds. The Turbinia Company went on to build two 30-knot (55.6 kmph) destroyers of 15,000 horsepower (11,190 kw) with this arrangement. The greatest gain was found in extending the use of turbines to vessels of slow speed.

The introduction of the turbine was the climax of the development of the steamship. The turbine superseded the reciprocating engine at sea. In 1904 the Cunard Line installed turbines in its new ships, the *Lusitania* and *Mauretania*. By 1904 twenty-six ships were powered by Parsons's direct-drive steam turbines, including *Mauretania*, *Titanic* and HMS *Dreadnought*. *Mauretania*, like many of these pioneering ships, was to be long remembered as a legend. She was the first passenger vessel to be fitted with the new steam turbine and she was the largest, fastest and also one of the most reliable liners of her time. All contemporary liners were made in comparison to her. The contract to build her was the result of an agreement in 1903 between Cunard and Parliament that two large passenger ships should be created to re-establish British supremacy in the Atlantic. There were stipulations that the vessels had to be made available to the Admiralty in times of war and that each vessel was to maintain a speed of 24–25 knots (44.5 –46.3 kmph).

Mauretania was launched for sea trials on the River Tyne in September 1906 amid scenes of great jubilation among the Tyneside craftsmen. After flawless trials she left Liverpool on 16 November 1907 bound for New York. There were more than 50,000 cheering spectators. It took five days, eighteen hours and seventeen minutes for the crossing at an average speed of 21–22 knots (38.9–40.1 kmph). In September 1909 *Mauretania* claimed the record for the fastest westbound crossing, which she held for over twenty years. It was a tribute to her as an engineering feat. During her period of service she was consistently reliable and on time, earning herself a reputation she would keep until the end of her career.

Speed wasn't her only strong point; *Mauretania* offered every luxury to be found afloat. The public rooms were graced with gilded Edwardian elegance, the decoration a rich assortment of fine wood-work. There was a sweeping grand staircase; electric lifts for first-class passengers; and a two-storey dining saloon featuring a domed ceiling adorned with the signs of the Zodiac. As reflected in much of society at the time, the extravagance stopped with the first class. The second and third classes were a distinct contrast. Fares for the first class could reach £200, compared to second-class at £10 and even less for third.

In 1914, with the events of the First World War, *Mauretania* was requisitioned by the British Admiralty and in 1915 she was converted for use as a troopship, ferrying troops to the European fronts. She sur-vived the wartime service where other ships fell victim to enemy guns and mines. In May 1919 she was returned to England to be restored to her pre-war condition but the war had taken its toll on the turbines and she was slower than before. She continued in service until 1935 when she made her final departure from Southampton and headed for the breaker's yard at Rosyth.

The *Mauretania*'s sister ship *Lusitania* was launched in 1907 and was the largest ship in the world at 787 feet (240 m) long and 31,550 tons. Her turbine engines enabled her to reach a speed of 25 knots (46.3 kmph), faster than other ships. In 1914, with the First World War underway, *Lusitania* and other transatlantic liners were at risk from German U-boats. On 16 January 1915 in choppy seas on the way to Queenstown, Ireland, the ship was running from possible German subs. To try to keep his vessel safe the captain raised the American flag. America was still neutral at this time and the event became world news. But on 17 April 1915, about 20 miles (32 km) off the Old Head of Kinsale, the ship was torpedoed by a U-boat. There was a second internal explosion and the ship sank, taking 1,198 people with her. It was this event that brought the United States into the First World War.

Altogether there were 300–400 ship-building firms on the Clyde, which were responsible for about 30,000 vessels altogether. At its peak in 1913 the river produced 370 ships. The majority were steamships, from steam launches to battleships, such as HMS *Hood*, and many famous liners. By the 1920s turbine-driven liners had taken over the world's shipping routes. Multiple cylinders were added to reciprocat-ing engines to take full advantage of the expansion of steam. The steam turbine virtually replaced the older reciprocating steam engine on major vessels. On the seas the turbine-driven liner represented the high point for overseas passenger travel. Turbines meant that ships were not only bigger than they had ever been before, but were also faster. The White Star and the French Line, among others, were competing to make the biggest and best liners, but the Cunard Line was the leader. The *Queen Elizabeth* and *Queen Mary* created a way of life that had never been experienced before.

The *Queen Elizabeth* was the second of two super-liners to be built by Cunard for the New York service. She was launched in September 1938 and was due to be fitted out and completed for spring 1940, but the outbreak of the Second World War on 3 September caused a change of plan. She was painted grey and her maiden voyage cancelled. She was thought to be at risk from German bombers and was also occupying a berth needed for warships, so she sailed off to New York. In March 1940 four of the world's greatest liners, *Mauretania*, *Normandie*, *Queen Elizabeth* and *Queen Mary*, were berthed alongside each other. During the war they were used to transport troops. By June 1946 *Queen Elizabeth* was back at Southampton for interior refurbishment and she made her first passenger voyage to New York on 16 October 1946. Despite being a huge success, the *Queen Elizabeth* never broke any speed records. This was done by the *Queen Mary* and later by the *United States*.

In spite of the fact that the steam turbine had ruled the ocean waves for over forty years, the old-style paddle-steamers didn't disappear completely. As late as the 1940s they were still building paddle-steam-ers on the Clyde. The *Waverley* was the last sea-going example in the world and it is one of only a very small number of craft that still survive for us to experience what it was like to go to sea on a real paddle-steamer. This lovely little ship carries on a very long tradition of paddle-steamers being used both for pleasure trips and, particularly in Scotland, as an important commuter link. She was originally built by A. and J. Inglis of Glasgow in 1947 for the London and North-Eastern Railway, later becoming part of the Caledonian Steam Packet

Company. She was fitted with a triple-expansion diagonal engine supplied with steam from a coal-fired double-ended boiler. All of the secondary and deck machinery was also powered by steam and the vessel was capable of going at a speed of 18.5 knots (34.2 kmph). *Waverley's* final season as a commercial vessel was in 1973 for Caledonian MacBrayne. But, thanks to the efforts of the Paddle-steamer Preservation Society, she continues to operate under the Waverley Steam Navigation Company and is the last sea-going paddle-steamer in the world. In the summer months she still plies the waters around the British coastline as a pleasure steamer, particularly old steamer strongholds such as the Bristol Channel and the Clyde.

Kingswear Castle is another paddle-steamer that has managed to escape the scrap heap and stay in active service today as an excursion steamer. Built in 1924 by Philip and Son of Dartmouth, she was the last paddle-steamer to be built for service on the River Dart and spent the summer days paddling between Kingswear in Dartmouth and Totnes with her almost identical sister ships *Totnes Castle* and *Compton Castle*. The steamer was built to replace an earlier *Kingswear Castle* and the main compound steam engine and other bits and pieces are taken from her 1904 predecessor. You could say that *Kingswear Castle* has been the lucky one, as *Compton Castle* is now a flower shop and café at Truro and *Totnes Castle* languishes beneath the English Channel.

During the Second World War *Kingswear Castle* was loaned out to the American Navy and used as a liberty ship at Dartmouth. She retained her bright peacetime colours and was quite a contrast against the grey of the warships. By the 1960s the popularity of seaside holidays and paddle-steamer cruises was well and truly in decline and the ship was withdrawn in 1965. After a spell on the Isle of Wight in 1971 she was towed to the River Medway in Kent for restoration, returning to service in 1985. Today you can visit the steamer at her base at the Historic Dockyard at Chatham or join her for one of her paddle cruises on the Medway and Thames throughout the summer months.

Top: The launch of Brunel's *SS Great Britain* in July 1843. It was the first big ocean-going vessel consructed from iron and driven by a steam-powered propeller.
Above: The invention of the steam hammer by James Naysmith at Patricroft near Manchester took the human effort out of the process of forging wrought iron and steel.

Left: This old photo shows Brunel (second right) and his colleagues involved in building the SS *Great Eastern*. The ship was by far the largest that had been built up to then and the worry caused by its construction brought about Brunel's early death.

Below: The SS *Great Eastern*. The great ship, four times the size of the SS *Great Britain* was built in 1858. She was 692 feet long (211 m) and carried 4000 passengers and was powered by both paddle-wheels and a screw propeller.

Opposite top: The speed with which the marine turbine was taken up is illustrated in this photo which shows the first turbine vessel *Turbania*, alongside the turbine-driven liner *Mauretania* which was completed only thirteen years later.

Opposite below: Two posters, advertizing the services of the great shipping lines of the early 20th century including the ill-fated *Titanic*.

Above: The launch of Cunard's super-liner *Queen Elizabeth* in September 1938.
Opposite: The record breaking *United States* launched in 1951. Like the *Queen Elizabeth* she was propelled by steam turbines.

Previous page: Paplewick pumping station provided water for the city of Nottingham. The interior shows the Victorian passion for ornate decoration. Above: A 1913 *Stanley Steamer*. The 1906 version of this steam-driven car reached over 127 miles (204 km) per hour. New evironmentally friendly designs for steam-powered cars are now being developed which could push this record up to 200 miles per hour (322 kmph).

CHAPTER SIX

THE AGE OF THE STEAM TURBINE

Charles Parsons had revolutionized marine propulsion with his invention of the steam turbine. But his work was to have an even greater impact on the provision of power for land transport, industry, home and office, which we still rely on today. Although steam engines of all types remained in use until the 1960s, from the late 1880s onwards the reciprocating steam engine began to give way to the steam turbine, with its inventor Charles Parsons following in the footsteps of Newcomen, Watt and Trevithick as one of the great figures in the history of steam power. In the 1880s, when Parsons was at university, the Industrial Revolution was in full flow and great reciprocating steam engines of one form or another mainly powered it. By this time, generating large amounts of power to drive the wheels of industry was posing a difficult problem. A lot of machinery was driven by bevelled cogwheels and shafting, and the noise was horrific. It got so bad that a generating station in Manchester actually closed down because of complaints about the racket that radiated from it during the course of the generation process.

Large steam engines drove factory machinery all over Britain. The engines were connected to machines by line shafting, which is a complex system of belts and pulleys that transmits power from one engine to many machines. The steam engine, which provided the power, would usually be in a separate engine house adjoining the factory. Now that these things are all gone it's hard for people to imagine how noisy they were. A friend of mine who was the chief mechanical engineer for a textile firm in Lancashire, called Vantona, used to tell me tales about when he had to go round repairing steam engines. On one occasion it was the middle of the night and they thought they'd ironed out the problem with the steam engine, which had a great deal of bevel gearing in its transmission to different parts of the works. They decided they would give it a trial run and started it up. The next thing they knew there were about twenty people outside the mill gates – they had been woken up by the noise of the gearing and thought it was seven o'clock and time to go to work!

But the engine itself didn't always cause the noise. Another interesting tale that my friend told me is about a repair job on a great flywheel on a steam engine. Because of the amount of draught that was generated from the spokes passing by, they boarded in these flywheels with rather beautiful tapering boards, which were wide at the rim end and narrow at the centre or the axle end of it. To get at the big nuts and bolts that held all the sections of the flywheel together they had to take a few boards off and get inside. They tightened up all these bolts, put the boards back and started the engine up. There was a great deal of rumbling and bumping coming from it and they thought somebody had left something inside. So they took the boards off again and did an investigation and found it was the works cat that had got inside. They had boarded him in and he'd been going round with the flywheel. Unfortunately he was dead. Rather funny in some ways, but not for the cat.

Of course all the racket made by steam engines in mills and factories led to the quest to find something that didn't make as much noise. The answer was electricity. Throughout the second half of the 1800s, electric generators and motors started to be built and electricity began to be used for driving factory machinery instead of steam. It changed the whole concept of powering all kinds of equipment. Up to this time the belts, pulleys and gears were the only way to take energy from a point of generation and deliver it to a point of use at some distance. Sooner or later this possibility of delivering energy to a motor over electric conductors was due to change a substantial part of the work done.

The beginnings of the age of electricity were back in the 1830s when the railway pioneers like George and Robert Stephenson were changing the face of the country. The development of electricity as our major source of power is inextricably linked with steam power. Michael Faraday, born in 1791, was a pioneer of scientific discovery.

In 1831 he began his great series of experiments in which he discovered electromagnetic induction, which would form the basis of modern electromagnetic technology. He demonstrated that moving a magnet through a coil of copper wire could produce an electric current. This was the first generator. After reading about his work, a young Frenchman called Hippolyte Pixii constructed an electric generator that utilized the rotary motion between magnet and coil rather than Faraday's to-and-fro motion in a straight line. All the generators in power stations today are direct descendants of the machine developed by Pixii from Faraday's first principles.

The first public supply of electricity was in 1881 at Godalming in Surrey for street lighting. The town council considered electricity as an alternative to gas when their contract for gas lighting expired. What probably swayed their opinion was that the electric bid was £195, which was £15 less than the gas bid. The source of power for the generator was one of the waterwheels at a local leather-dressing mill, half a mile from the town centre.

The next year, 1882, saw the birth of purpose-built power stations. On 12 January Thomas Edison opened the Edison Electric Light Station at No. 57 Holborn Viaduct in London. Soon after, on 27 February, the Hammond Electric Light Company opened the Brighton power station, which claims to be the first permanent and viable public power supply. By 1892 it was realized that electricity could be used for heating and two years later it was possible to 'cook electric'. In 1918 electric washing machines became available and in the following year the refrigerator appeared. By this time electricity had been accepted as the energy of the future and word was getting around – everyone wanted it.

But the thing that made possible the mass supply of electricity was steam. Charles Parsons realized the need for a rotary form of power to generate electricity: in other words, one spindle directly on to a dynamo. The dynamo then converts mechanical energy into electrical energy by means of electromagnetic induction. The steam turbine that he invented provided the rotary form of power that was needed. After university he had served his time as an apprentice at the Elswick works of W. G. Armstrong in Newcastle upon Tyne, where they had worked on methods of generating electricity. An apprenticeship like this for a young man of his social class was rather unusual, but he had what was called the 'premium' apprenticeship, which eventually would have led to a managerial position. In 1884 he left Armstrong's to become the junior partner for Clark and Chapman. It became Clark, Chapman and Parsons and there he perfected his first multi-stage/blade reaction turbine. When Parsons introduced his revolutionary steam turbine it was along with an integrated high-speed dynamo, which converted mechanical energy into electrical energy by means of electromagnetic induction. Parsons was on the threshold of revolutionizing power generation using steam, and his work was to be key to many of the twentieth century's accomplishments. With his turbine Parsons made sure that steam would continue to be used in an age of electricity.

As well as being employed for generating electricity and for marine propulsion Parsons's turbines also started to be used for working blast-furnace blowers and centrifugal pumps. They were cleaner and more efficient than reciprocating engines and, as the turbines used the exhaust steam from other engines, there were less clouds of steam blowing off to waste. The first turbine to be used in a rolling mill was a 750-horsepower (560 kw) exhaust turbine in Scotland. It revolved at 2,000 revolutions per minute. With a double reduction of helical gears it drove the mill at 70 revolutions. A flywheel also helped to equalize the speed. Parsons predicted that from this moment the use of land and marine turbines would steadily increase and improvements would continue to be made to increase their efficiency.

Almost all the electricity we use in the UK today comes from generators driven by steam turbines. The steam is obtained by burning fuels such as coal, oil and gas or from nuclear reaction. The heat is used to turn water into steam and it is the power of the steam, that makes a turbine spin. The idea of using the expansion of steam to make a machine turn is hundreds of years old. Everybody had a go at it. But really, the deep knowledge and the understanding of steam and its expansion and the materials needed to build a practical steam turbine were all put together and developed by Charles Parsons. I suppose you could say that Charles Parsons and his steam turbine are to the twentieth century what James Watt and his engine were to the nineteenth century. Everybody, of course, has heard of Watt but not many people have heard of Parsons. Parsons was a very ingenious man. He took out over 300 different patents for his inventions. He was also a family man and he amused his children by making all manner of creations like helicopters and three-wheel go-carts. However, his real claim to fame was the steam turbine and the generation of electricity, which is still done in exactly the same way to this day.

The introduction of electricity into industry was a great advance, changing the whole concept of powering all kinds of equipment. It enabled engineers to do away with hundreds of miles of line shafting and belts and all the unnecessary friction that was caused from the main source of power, like the steam engine at the end of the line. As early as the 1900s in America they were critical of the business of using a single steam engine to drive a group of machines. Factories became filled with individually driven machines, like a lathe with an electric motor stuck on the end of it or an electric motor on the end of a shaft. The beauty of this was the fact that you weren't wasting any energy. Before the turbine, if you had a great line shaft that was being turned by a steam engine, it was on the go all the time. Of course the fires were burning, the steam was being generated and the wheels were all going round for nothing until you moved the belt shifter and got the lathe going. With a steam turbine, when you press the button the machine starts and when you depress the button the machine stops. It is as simple and as efficient as that.

Although the introduction of electricity on to the industrial scene sounded the death knell for large reciprocating steam engines, they didn't disappear that quickly. For a time, instead of driving the whole works by belts and shafts, they would still have a steam engine, generate electricity and then transfer the electricity along wires to individual motors and machines. This was all very well until along came the great turbine-driven power stations, which produced electricity much more cheaply than a steam engine in a works could do. Eventually the steam engines in industry and the private steam turbines disappeared in favour of a big fat cable running underneath the pavement. In spite of this the old-style steam engine, including the beam engine, survived in some industries until well into the second half of the twentieth century.

Because it provided such an efficient method of pumping water, the beam engine became the basic working machine of the water industry and it was with the building of pumping stations in the nineteenth century that beam-engine technology reached its peak. Many of the pumping stations that were built then survived all over England in beautiful ornate engine rooms fitted out with all the trappings you might expect to find in a rather grand town hall. Some of them were like Greek palaces with ornamental ironwork, gold leaf and fancy painting. They were beautiful creations, which of course eventually became redundant and all ended up being replaced by an electric rotary pump. But the original beam engines did the job so well that many of them continued to provide the main source of power in the water industry until well into the 1960s.

One that lasted until this time was the Ryhope Pumping Station just outside Sunderland. But at 3 pm on 1 July 1967 a century of water pumping by beam engines came to an end at Ryhope – the last steam pumping station to be used by the Sunderland and South Shields Water Company. Fortunately, soon after completion of its working life, a group of enthusiasts got together to preserve the station in working order for the benefit of anybody who wanted to experience the unique sight, sound and smell of a huge beam engine in motion. Ryhope has two massive compound beam engines and a range of three Lancashire boilers. The high standard of the original design and manufacture and the subsequent maintenance over their 100-year working life left the engines in perfect condition and they are now among the finest examples of working beam engines to be seen in Britain.

London also has its own magnificent beam engines at Kew Bridge Steam Museum, which boasts the largest collection of static steam engines in the world. It is housed in a former pumping station which belonged to the Metropolitan Water Board and, like so many of the Victorian pumping stations, there is a great style about it. Inside this collection of Grade I and Grade II listed buildings, which include the original engine rooms and boiler room, there are nine steam pumping engines of varying type and design. Many are in steam every weekend, including the Grand Junction 90, the massive Cornish beam engine manufactured by Harvey's of Hayle, which pumped water to west

London for over a century. It is, they claim, the largest working beam engine in the world and it was able to pump water at the rate of 717 gallons (3,260 litres) at every single stroke. Also on show is the oldest of the original Kew engines – a Boulton and Watt dating from 1820.

On the railways, although the first electric trains were in operation by the early 1900s, steam continued to flourish, and the period from about 1900 to 1940 was a golden age when the steam locomotive reached its peak of perfection, in Britain at least. The railway was seen as the pulse of the nation and was the primary form of transport for moving freight and people. The modest locomotive designs of the nineteenth century were surpassed by larger, heavier and more powerful engines in the twentieth. By the 1920s there was more demand for passenger locomotives. The Southern Railway introduced the four-cylinder Lord Nelsons that were able to pull a 500-ton train at almost a mile a minute. In 1922 H. N. (later Sir Nigel) Gresley introduced his own design, of the *Pacific*, to the Great Northern Railway, which merged with several others in 1923 to form the London and North-Eastern Railway. The *Pacific* was never surpassed in size or power; in fact it could be said Gresley's A4s were the Concordes of their day. In 1938 one of his *Pacifics* named *Mallard* attained the world speed record for steam traction of 129 miles per hour (208 kmph) while it was on a test run. It was a magnificent piece of machinery. Gresley became a pioneer of railway streamlining and long-distance non-stop passenger expresses. For the London– Edinburgh run he built tenders with corridors to enable crews to be relieved while the train was in motion.

There is a view that the steam locomotive was replaced by diesels and electrics because it was slow. However, as many of the services today are not much faster than steam was fifty years ago, this was obviously not the case. In fact it was as long ago as 1904 that a speed of over 100 miles per hour (161 kmph) was registered by the Great Western locomotive *City of Truro*. But it was in the 1930s that there were record-breaking speed runs all over the country, especially down the east and west coast main lines in the challenge for the fastest way to Scotland from London. It was all quite exciting, this time of the great races. The London, Midland and Scottish record of 114 miles per hour (183.5 kmph) on the approaches to Crewe in 1937 held for just over one year. Alas, in this effort the train approached Crewe station at approximately 65 miles per hour (105 kmph) and the braking that was necessary to stop at the platform signal resulted in smashed crockery in the dining car.

It was only one year and four days later that the London and North-Eastern Railway with *Mallard* achieved 126 miles per hour (203 kmph) between Grantham and Peterborough – a record that has never broken by a steam locomotive. *Mallard* was one of many Gresley class A4 steam engines built by LNER in the 1930s, for high-speed passenger transport along the east coast mainline (London–Edinburgh). Gresley's design for the A4s, incorporating sleek curves, was both beautiful and functional. It was inspired by the Bugatti railcars in France.

The first of Gresley's A4 locos rolled out of Doncaster works in 1935, but as soon as they started running, a major problem was identified. The engine was so fast that the old-style braking system that had been in use until this time was inadequate. So the Westinghouse Brake and Signal Company had to develop a new system. Two years later *Mallard* was selected to do the test runs for its new quick-service vacuum braking system. It was one of these tests that Gresley decided offered an ideal opportunity to push the locomotive to its limits and win back the British speed record, which had been set so recently by the rival London, Midland and Scottish Railway. They might even be able to break the world record, which, by this time, was held by the Germans with a speed of 125 miles per hour (201 kmph). So, on 3 July 1938 *Mallard* headed south from Grantham station pulling six coaches and a dynamometer car for measuring speed and power in search of the record. The driver, Joe Duddington, and his fireman, Tommy Bray, built speed up steadily and the train was soon thundering along at 122 miles per hour (196 kmph). Eventually *Mallard* hit 126 miles per hour (203 kmph) and held the speed for 306 yards (280 m) before easing back for the approach to Peterborough. After her record-breaking run *Mallard* was put to work, hauling express trains on the east coast main line until she was retired from service in 1963, having travelled nearly 1½ million miles. Sadly, she isn't able to steam now, but you can see her along with the dynamometer car at the National Railway Museum in York.

In France there was a man called André Chapelon who put France and Europe at the forefront of the develpment of the steam engine from the 1930s. Outside of the United States, Chapelon was by far the most innovative steam loco design engineer. Under his supervision French locos developed the highest ratings for thermal efficiency, fuel economy, and power-to-weight ratios.

The last steam locomotive to be built in Britain was the mixed-traffic *Evening Star*, which was designed to haul passenger and goods trains. This locomotive, which can now also be seen at the National Railway Museum, was built at Swindon works in 1960. But on the ocean, great steam-turbine-powered liners were still being built even later than this. After nearly 120 years the Cunard Line ruled the steamship lines. Its *Queen Mary* and *Queen Elizabeth* were the two most famous ships on the sea, but they were built before the Second World War and, by the dawn of the 1960s, were showing their age. As most people were now crossing the Atlantic by plane, it was questionable as to whether or not it was worth replacing them. The ocean liners were becoming increasingly expensive to operate and it was clear that they were going the way of the dinosaur.

Still, Cunard took a great gamble with a new breed of passenger ship: a transatlantic liner as well as an island cruise ship that would cost $80 million. Once the *Elizabeth* and *Mary* retired, this vessel would make or break Cunard, and the only way the company could succeed was if it adapted to the changing times. It wasn't easy for a firm that had established many of the traditions of the industry. *Queen Elizabeth II*'s keel was laid in June of 1965 in the same slipway where the *Queen Mary* had been built thirty years earlier.

QEII made her first crossing in May of 1969 – it was just two months before *Apollo 11* would land on the moon. In a time when man was preparing to go to the moon, crossing the ocean over the course of days in a steamship seemed prehistoric! She travelled at an average speed of 28.02 knots (51.9 kmph), taking four days, sixteen hours and thirty-five minutes. She was welcomed to New York with a traditional fanfare, but most people realized that this was the last time a new liner would steam in to the harbour. She was, indeed, the last of her breed. *QEII* was not the largest liner ever built, or the fastest. Those honours went to the *France* and the *United States* respectively. Nonetheless, she enjoyed all the latest technology the age had to offer. She was built at the shipyards of John Brown and Company of Glasgow, who built liners for Cunard as far back as 1900 with the 14,200-ton *Saxonia*. But this ship was to be different and they had to disregard all their formulae that had worked so well for so long to create an all-new interpretation of the passenger liner.

One of the most ingenious innovations on *QEII* was her main funnel. Since the earliest days of steamship travel, exhaust from the stack had always been a problem. The soot and fumes annoyed passengers, dirtied their clothes and irritated the eyes, making the only large open area unpleasant. On *QEII* the problem would have been even worse because the entire area was to be enclosed with tall windscreens to protect the pools and sun decks from the ocean breeze, and the fumes would not be able to escape. After lengthy tests, the wind scoop at the base of the funnel was introduced. As the ship moves forward, air is channelled up the scoop and helps push the exhaust fumes up and away to clear the decks.

On the roads, although it might surprise some people, steam was still around well into my lifetime. From the early days of the twentieth century the steam wagon or lorry was developed for road haulage of a more mundane type than that of the big traction engine, for goods from factories, like bales of cotton. In the early days the steam wagon looked like a flat horse cart, with a steam engine and cab with no window-panes. If the rain was coming straight down you were dry, but if it was coming sideways on you probably got quite wet. Steam wagons had very feeble speeds like 12 miles an hour (19 kmph) in the country and 5 miles an hour (8 kmph) in town. But they were developed to a very high degree and by around 1936 they were brilliant. Later models were fitted with pneumatic tyres and could reach speeds of 60 miles per hour (97 kmph). They made the diesel wagons and the early petrol wagons look puny.

When I was a little lad the Bleachers' Association at Manchester had a fleet of these things called Sentinel Steam Wagons, which were made by a company called Alley and McLellan from Glasgow. These steam wagons would do 40 miles an hour (64 kmph) with a trailer full of rolls of cloth; and big rolls of cloth are really heavy. They used to come down the middle of Manchester Road in Bolton past Burnden Park football ground like an express train with the safety valves blowing out at the top and the driver hanging out of the cab looking all smutty and black. You got out of the way when you saw one of these coming. They'd a rather strange way of putting coal on. The boiler is like a dustbin with a lid on top. When you lift the lid off, all the heat and the muck comes out in your face and it gets very hot. Then they altered the Road Traffic Act and it became uneconomical to carry on with the steam wagon. As efficient and powerful as it was, the steam wagon was slowly but surely abandoned.

There are three main reasons why so many have survived. First, they were so good and so powerful that, if you had great steel works with a lot of internal roads, you could keep your steam wagon and use it on your road system. Another reason is that if you had a road-making vehicle you didn't pay any tax on it. So a lot of what had been flat-backed steam wagons had big tar boilers put on the back. Finally, you could even leave it as a wagon. As long as you didn't do anything other than move road stone with it, you didn't have to pay any tax. That's the reason why a lot of steam wagons survived. The usage of the traction engine and the fairground engine survived up to about 1950. But if it hadn't been for the work of the preservationists and the restoration men they would undoubtedly have gone forever. Most people would probably be surprised to learn that there are still nearly 4,000 steam-driven road vehicles in Britain.

Steam is certainly still alive and well in my back garden. The boiler I have makes steam for turning a steam engine round and that engine works no less than fifteen machines. It comes in handy for lots of occasions and particularly for repairs to the traction engine. I've been at it now for twenty-seven years and after two divorces it's almost there – just a little bit more finance and time and I could complete it. I've made new piston rods myself and new covers and valve rods for the valve chest covers and taken off all the corroded parts to get them back looking like new – some of them even better than new. Now I've finished the boiler tests and got it to over 200 psi it's almost a kit of parts that's ready for assembly. It will be an unbelievable sense of achievement when I do get it finished because by then I will have built the whole thing myself from scratch with a complete new boiler and all the parts hand-made.

Although steam did stay around, in general throughout the twentieth century transport and industry turned more and more to electrical power. But steam didn't go away, because it was still at the heart of the power-generating process. And so it continues right up to this day. Even in a modern nuclear power station the steam engine is still the main thing. Without the use of a steam engine, nuclear energy could not be harnessed for useful work, because a nuclear reactor does not directly generate either mechanical or electrical energy. The nuclear reactor just gets hot and it is the steam engine that converts that heat to drive the generator or the turbine. The basic process of nuclear power is that the nucleus of the atom splits up and gives off energy. This energy is used to heat water and produce steam, which pushes a turbine. This is connected to a great generator that converts the mechanical energy of the turbine into electrical energy.

The main difference between a coal-fired power station and a nuclear power station is that a nuclear plant uses uranium contained in metal fuel rods instead of coal to heat water and make the steam. Uranium is formed into ceramic pellets and placed in metal tubes called fuel rods. In pressurized water reactors about 51,000 fuel rods are placed in the reactor vessel to make up the core – the part of the plant that produces heat. Nuclear fission (when a uranium atom splits) gives off energy in the form of heat. Controlled rods and borated water are used to regulate the heat-producing process. The borated water speeds up or slows down the fission process, and the control rods shut down the reaction when they are inserted between the fuel rods. The water is heated to about 340°C (640°F). It is kept under high pressure to prevent it from boiling as it travels to tubes inside four steam generators. A secondary source of water passes around the outside of the tubes in the steam generators. The heat from the water inside the tubes is transferred to the secondary source of water, which boils and turns to steam. The steam formed in the generators is piped into the main turbine, where the force turns the turbine blades. The turbine is connected to an electric generator by a rotating shaft. As the turbine blades begin to spin, a magnet inside the generator also turns, and that produces electricity.

Once the steam has been used to drive the main turbine, the low-energy steam is converted back to water by circulating around tubes (carrying cool water from an adjacent lake) in a large box-like structure called a condenser. The condensed steam, now water, is pumped to the steam generators to repeat the cycle. The water in the condenser tubes picks up heat from the steam passing around the outside of the tubes. This heated water may be passed through a 460-foot-high (140-m-high) cooling tower before being returned to the lake or reused in the plant. The three water systems are separated from each other to ensure that radioactive water does not mix with non-radioactive.

At the Science Museum in London you can see a life-size replica of part of a nuclear reactor core. It's based on those at Heysham, Lancaster and Torness near Dunbar, East Lothian. The fuel is uranium dioxide, contained in fuel elements, which are loaded into channels in the graphite core. In operation the reactor is filled with carbon dioxide gas at high temperature and pressure. It acts as a 'coolant' by carrying heat to the boilers where it heats up the water and is used to produce steam. That steam is used to produce electricity in exactly the same way Charles Parsons devised more than a century ago.

The first nuclear reactor to be built in this country was at Harwell in Oxfordshire. It began operating in August 1947 and was used for research on reactor design. In 1956 the world's first large scale nuclear power station opened at Calder Hall, which is now part of the huge nuclear plant at Sellafield in Cumbria. In the 1950s the demand for weapons-grade plutonium was increasing, and together with four reactors at Chapelcross in Scotland, the reactors in Calder Hall were to supply the necessary quantity. The reactors at Calder Hall were the first of a new generation of British reactors that later came to be called Magnox reactors. In total, twenty-six such reactors were built in the UK. Except for Calder Hall and its sister power plant, Chapelcross, all of these reactors were constructed in the period between 1960 and 1970. Now, with the imminent closure of Calder Hall and Chapelcross, only eight Magnox reactors will remain in operation.

The history of the steam engine and the steam turbine is very important when it comes to nuclear energy, for, as already stated, nuclear energy is really only another way of boiling water. Today in the UK, nuclear power stations generate about a quarter of our electricity. This will be cut to 17 per cent when the remaining stations reach the end of their life and close in 2016. The major problem that we have with nuclear power is the waste material that comes from it, which of course is radioactive and highly dangerous. There have been many disasters like that at Chernobyl in the then USSR and other places, which have caused radioactive leaks. In my opinion the man who discovers the way to make radioactive waste safe will become another of our great heroes on this planet.

Even now, there's a lot more use of steam than many people imagine. Some companies have continued to push the boundaries of steam turbine power beyond the days of Queen Victoria right up to the present day and there are many, many innovative uses of steam turbines to be found all over the world today. Renewable energy is one area in which steam turbines can be used in some interesting ways. One of the most environmentally friendly and clever uses is in waste-to-energy projects. Instead of simply getting rid of waste produced by homes and businesses these turbines turn it into something extremely useful – power. There is, for example, a steam turbine at work in Crymlyn Burrows in south Wales, which uses waste from homes and businesses to generate electricity. About half of the 4.5 mw of electricity generated is used on the site itself, which includes a recycling and composting programme. The remainder is used by the borough council in council buildings and for street lighting. At a waste-to-energy plant in Fawley, Southampton, the turbine-generated electricity produced from 60,000 tons of waste per year is enough to provide 12,000 homes with all the power they need.

Steam turbines can even help us to generate energy from sewage. In most countries there are laws that prohibit the dumping of raw sewage, so it has to undergo a treatment process called the 'digestion process'. After this, what remains is a sewage sludge, which can be disposed of in a variety of ways, but if it is dried into 'cakes' or briquettes, it can be incinerated. At one sewage plant in the UK a power station has been constructed that uses dried sewage briquettes to produce power as a supplementary fuel for its boiler.

It's surprising to see where the steam turbine is being used as an environmentally friendly method of producing energy. It's quite ironic, for instance, that Ford Motor Company, the home of the internal combustion engine, uses a steam turbo-generator in a way that helps it use energy more efficiently in an environmentally friendly way. At its car-manufacturing plant in Dagenham, Essex, a steam turbo-generator generates electricity from previously wasted energy. A turbo-generator working in conjunction with a pressure-reducing valve takes in the high-pressure steam and generates 1.6 mw of electricity to be used by the car plant. The system has drastically reduced the amount of energy the company loses and has to buy in. Perhaps Ford will start manufacturing a steam-powered car next.

The idea for a steam-powered car isn't as far-fetched as you might imagine. When most people think of steam-powered vehicles they imagine great ponderous road rollers or traction engines belching out clouds of smoke. But if you think steam is old-fashioned, think again. Since the beginning of the twentieth century we have become used to the dominance of the internal combustion engine to power our road vehicles. We tend to take this for granted and assume it is the best way to do things. But as early as 1906 a man called Fred Marriott drove a steam-powered vehicle built by the Stanley Brothers, which reached the incredible speed of 127.6 miles per hour (205.4 kmph). The cigar-shaped *Stanley Steamer* was a triumph of engineering at the time. So the

Above: A *Stanley Steamer* of 1906.

technology was certainly around to develop steam-powered cars and some people argue that it was only because of shifts in the financial markets, clever advertising and business pressures that the petrol engine took over.

Whether or not these were the reasons, the internal combustion engine did take over and, apart from the odd steam-powered lorry that I remember when I was a lad, not very much happened in the field of steam-powered road vehicles after the exploits of the *Stanley Steamer*. Then in 1969 the state of California began to experiment with the notion of creating an environmentally friendly public bus service and to achieve their aim they looked at the idea of using steam-powered vehicles. The idea isn't as strange as it sounds because, whereas the internal combustion engine relies upon highly refined hydrocarbon fuels which pollute the atmosphere, an external combustion engine such as a steam engine is not fuel-specific. This means that any fuel can be used including the cleanest and most ecologically friendly fuel, direct sunlight. Several steam turbines were developed for the project, but it never really got anywhere. However, during the mid-1980s one of these turbines found its way into the hands of a team who used it in a car they built to make an attempt on the world land-speed record for a steam-powered vehicle. The car they designed succeeded in reaching speeds of 145.607 miles per hour (234.332 kmph).

Now a dedicated British team of engineers and designers has taken on the challenge. They are aiming to show us this exciting, modern steam technology by building a new car for a British attempt on the world land-speed record for a steam-powered vehicle. The aim is to take the record first to 150 miles per hour (241 kmph) and then move up to crack the 200-miles-per-hour (321-kmph) barrier. Apart from the record itself, the wider aim is to influence a new generation of engineers and designers to take an ecologically friendly approach to solving problems and to remember that, no matter how old the technology, there are always new and better ways to put that technology to work for the benefit of mankind. The car they are building is called *Inspiration* and they hope that it will live up to its name, inspiring engineers, designers and members of the public to explore the amazing potential of cleaner and safer forms of transport. The external combustion steam engine designed for *Inspiration* has a low combustion pressure and an extremely clean-burning fuel. The process can be tightly controlled so that, although a hydrocarbon-fuelled external engine still produces carbon dioxide and water vapour, carbon monoxide emissions can be radically cut and almost no nitrogen oxide compounds are produced. So not only can steam-powered vehicles be very fast, they can also be very 'green'.

Design features, such as the *Inspiration*'s rear engine, rear-wheel drive, braking and suspension systems, share many similarities with the vehicles we drive around every day. The truly innovative thing about the car's design is its motive power. A 13-inch-diameter (33-cm-diameter) non-condensing turbine is fed at four nozzles from each of the four liquefied petroleum gas-(LPG)-fired boilers. The boilers will produce steam at 500 lbs per square inch (35 kg per cm²) and the turbine will in turn drive a gear train and the wheels at speeds of 3,000 revolutions per minute, taking the vehicle up to 200 miles per hour (321 kmph). The system is what is called total loss, which means that each run will use up the total amount of water the car carries and the exhaust steam is vented into the wake of the car. Despite all these complicated mechanics the whole thing is smooth and aerodynamic on the outside. The basic shape is called the 'Morelli' shape and, like the aerodynamic shapes of jet planes and high-performance cars and motorcycles, is intended to move the vehicle as quickly as possible through the air while using up the least amount of energy possible.

The project is exciting because it couples the wealth of steam knowledge gained from Victorian times onwards with some of the most advanced technologies known to man today. It could be a stepping-stone in the direction of transport technologies for the future and in the direction of a new Age of Steam. It's strange that one of the causes of the first Age of Steam coming to an end was all that black smoke polluting the atmosphere, but now, with the use of cleaner fuels, steam could be the answer to some of our major environmental problems. It all seems to have gone full circle. My only regret is that, if there is another Age of Steam, I probably won't be around to see it. Over the span of my lifetime, the first age has nearly finished and the new one, if it is to happen, won't have started.

WHERE TO SEE
STEAM ENGINES

SOUTH WEST

STATIONARY STEAM ENGINES

Cornish Mines and Engines at Poole tel: 01209 315027
www.trevithicktrust.com

Crofton Beam Engines tel: 01672 870300
www.crofton.ndo.co.uk
www.katrust.org

Levant Beam Engine tel: 01736 786156
www.nationaltrust.org.uk
http://freespace.virgin.net/levant.mine/frameset-1.htm

Newcomen Memorial Engine tel: 01803 834766
www.dartmouth.org.uk/newcomen.htm

Westonzoyland Pumping Station tel: 01823 257516
www.wzlet.org

Coldharbour Mill tel: 01884 840960
www.coldharbourmill.org.uk/Homepage.html

Poldark Mine Heritage Centre tel: 01326 573173
www.poldark-mine.co.uk

Wheal Martyn China Clay Heritage Centre tel: 01726 850362
www.wheal-martyn.com

RAILWAYS

Bodmin and Wenford Railway tel: 0845 1259678
www.bodminandwenfordrailway.com

East Somerset Railway tel: 01749 880417
www.eastsomersetrailway.org.uk

Steam Museum of the Great Western Railway tel: 01793 466646
www.steam-museum.org.uk

Lappa Valley Steam Railway tel: 01872 510317
www.lappavalley.co.uk

Launceston Steam Railway tel: 01566 775665

Paignton and Dartmouth Steam Railway tel: 01803 555872
www.paignton-steamrailway.co.uk

Swanage Railway tel: 01929 425800
www.swanagerailway.co.uk

SHIPS AND ENGINEERING

Bristol Industrial Museum tel: 0117 9251470
www.bristol-city.gov.uk/museums

SS Great Britain and Maritime Heritage Centre tel: 0117 9260680
www.ss-great-britain.com

HMS Warrior and Portsmouth Historic Dockyard
tel: 023 92861512
www.flagship.org.uk

SOUTH EAST

STATIONARY STEAM ENGINES

British Engineerium tel: 01273 559583
www.britishengineerium.com

Kew Bridge Steam Museum tel: 020 8568 4757
www.kbsm.org

Tower Bridge tel: 020 7403 3761
www.towerbridge.org.uk

The Crossness Engines tel: 020 8311 3711
www.crossness.org.uk

Markfield Beam Engine and Museum 020 8800 7061
http://freespace.virgin.net/lec.orm

Eastney Beam Engine House tel: 023 92827261
www.hants.gov.uk/discover/places/eastneypump.html

RAILWAYS

Bluebell Railway tel: 01825 722370
www.bluebellrailway.co.uk

Buckinghamshire Railway Centre tel: 01296 655720
www.bucksrailcentre.org.uk

Chinor and Princes Risborough Railway tel: 01844 353535
www.cprra.co.uk

Colne Valley Railway and Museum tel: 01787 461174
www.colnevalleyrailway.co.uk

East Anglian Railway Museum tel: 01206 242524
www.earm.co.uk

Isle of Wight Steam Railway tel: 01983 882204
www.iwsteamrailway.co.uk

Kent and East Sussex Railway tel: 01580 765155
www.kesr.org.uk

The Lavender Line tel: 01825 750515
www.lavender-line.co.uk

Leighton Buzzard Railway tel: 01525 373888
www.buzzrail.com

Mangapps Farm Railway Museum tel: 01621 784898
www.mangapps.co.uk

Watercress Line tel: 01962 733810
www.watercressline.co.uk

SHIPS AND ENGINEERING

Amberley Museum tel: 01798 831370
www.amberleymuseum.co.uk

Chatham Historic Dockyard tel: 01634 823807
www.chdt.org.uk

Hollycombe Steam Collection tel: 01428 724900
www.hollycombe.co.uk

Science Museum tel: 0870 8704771
www.nmsi.ac.uk

EASTERN

STATIONARY STEAM ENGINES

Stretham Old Engine tel: 01353 649210
www.ely.org.uk/soe/index.html

Cambridge Museum of Technology tel: 01223 368650
www.museumoftechnology.com

Thursford Collection tel: 01328 878477
www.norfolka22.co.uk/thursford/thursford.htm

RAILWAYS

Cleethorpes Coast Light Railway tel: 01472 604657
www.webmagix.demon.co.uk/cclr/

North Norfolk Railway – The Poppy Line tel: 01263 820800
www.nnrailway.co.uk

Wells and Walsingham Light Railway tel: 01328 710631

Bressingham Steam Museum tel: 01379 686903
www.bressingham.co.uk

Longshop Steam Museum tel: 01728 832189
www.longshop.care4free.net

CENTRAL

STATIONARY STEAM ENGINES

Abbey Pumping Station tel: 0116 2995111
www.leicestermuseums.ac.uk/museums/aps.html

Claymills Pumping Station tel: 01283 509929
www.claymills.org.uk

Dean Heritage Centre tel: 01594 822170
www.fweb.org.uk/deanmuseum

Etruria Industrial Museum tel: 01782 233144
www2002.stoke.gov.uk/museums/etruria/

Leawood Pumping House
www.grant2222.freeserve.co.uk/leahp.htm

Middleton Top Engine House tel: 01629 823204
www.grant2222.freeserve.co.uk/mtlhp.htm

Soho House Museum tel: 0121 5549122
www.bmag.org.uk/soho_house/

Think Tank tel: 0121 2022222
www.thinktank.ac

Black Country Living Museum tel: 0121 557 9643
www.bclm.co.uk

Peak District Mining Museum
www.peakmines.co.uk

Ironbridge Gorge Museums tel: 01952 432166
www.ironbridge.org.uk

RAILWAYS

Dean Forest Railway tel: 01594 843423
www.deanforestrailway.co.uk

Didcot Railway Centre tel: 01235 817200
www.didcotrailwaycentre.org.uk

Foxfield Steam Railway tel: 01782 396210
www.foxfieldrailway.co.uk

Great Central Railway tel: 01509 230726
www.gcrailway.co.uk

Midland Railway Centre tel: 01773 747674
www.midlandrailwaycentre.co.uk

Nottingham Transport and Heritage Centre tel: 0115 9405705
www.nthc.org.uk

Severn Valley Railway tel: 01299 403816
www.svr.co.uk

SHIPS AND ENGINEERING

National Waterways Museum tel: 01452 318200
www.nwm.org.uk

WALES

STATIONARY STEAM ENGINES

Kidwelly Industrial Museum tel: 01554 891078
www.llanegwad-carmarthen.co.uk/carmskidwellymuseum.html

Elliot Colliery tel: 02920 880011
www.caerphilly.gov.uk/historyandheritage/elliotcollierygroups.htm

RAILWAYS

Bala Lake Railway tel: 01678 540666
www.bala-lake-railway.co.uk

Brecon Mountain Railway tel: 01685 722988
www.breconmountainrailway.co.uk

Fairbourne and Barmouth Steam Railway tel: 01341 250362
www.fairbourne.freeserve.co.uk/fairrail

Vale of Rheidol Railway tel: 01970 625819
www.rheidolrailway.co.uk

Welsh Highland Railway tel: 01766 513402
www.whr.co.uk/enthus/index.html

Welshpool and Llanfair Light Railway tel: 01938 810441
www.wllr.org.uk

Lllanberis Lake Railway tel: 01286 870549
www.lake-railway.freeserve.co.uk

Llangollen Railway tel: 01978 860979
www.llangollen-railway.co.uk

Snowdon Mountain Railway tel: 0870 4580033
www.snowdonrailway.co.uk

Ffestiniog Railway tel: 01766 516024
www.festrail.co.uk

Talyllyn Railway tel: 01654 710472
www.talyllyn.co.uk

SHIPS AND ENGINEERING

Swansea Maritime and Industrial Museum tel: 01792 653763
www.swansea.gov.uk/culture/museums/maritime.htm

Waverley Paddle Steamer – Waverley Excursions
tel: 0845 1304647
www.waverleyexcursions.co.uk

NORTH WEST

STATIONARY STEAM ENGINES

Ellenroad Engine House tel: 01706 881952
www.ellenroad.org.uk

Wetheriggs Pottery tel: 01768 892733
www.wetheriggs-pottery.co.uk

Wigan Pier tel: 01942 323666
www.wlct.org/tourism/wiganpier/wiganpier.htm

Queen Street Mill tel: 01282 412555

Quarry Bank Mill tel: 01625 527468
www.nationaltrust.org.uk

Astley Green Colliery Museum
www.astleygreen.freeservers.com/Intro.htm

RAILWAYS

East Lancashire Railway tel: 0161 7647790
www.east-lancs-rly.co.uk

Ravenglass and Eskedale Railways tel: 01229 717171
www.ravenglass-railway.co.uk

Museum of Science and Industry In Manchester
tel: 0161 8322244
www.msim.org.uk

SHIPS AND ENGINEERING

Steam Yacht Gondola tel: 015394 41288
www.nationaltrust.co.uk

Windermere Steamboat Museum tel: 015394 45565
www.steamboat.co.uk

NORTH EAST

STATIONARY STEAM ENGINES

Elsecar tel: 01226 740203
www.barnsley.gov.uk/tourism/elsecar/index.asp

Ryhope Pumping Station
www.g3wte.demon.co.uk

Armley Mills Industrial Museum tel: 0113 2637861
www.leeds.gov.uk/armleymills/

Bradford Industrial Museum tel: 01274 435900
www.bradford.gov.uk

Calderdale Industrial Museum tel: 01422 358087

Kelham Island Industrial Museum tel: 0114 2722106
www.simt.co.uk

National Coal Mining Museum for England tel: 01924 848806
www.ncm.org.uk

Beamish, The North Of England Open Air Museum
tel: 0191 3704000
www.beamish.org.uk

Tees Cottage Pumping House
tel: 01325 487226
www.communigate.co.uk/ne/teescottagepumpingstation/index.phtml

RAILWAYS

Bowes Railway tel: 0191 4161847
www.bowesrailway.co.uk

Darlington Railway Centre and Museum tel: 01325 460532
www.drcm.org.uk

Embsay and Bolton Abbey Steam Railway tel: 01756 710614
www.embsayboltonabbeyrailway.org.uk

North Yorkshire Moors Railway tel: 01751 473535
www.nymr.demon.co.uk

Keighly and Worth Valley Railway tel: 01535 645214
www.kwvr.co.uk

Kirklees Light Railway tel: 01484 865727
www.kirkleeslightrailway.com

Middleton Railway tel: 0113 2710320
www.middletonrailway.org.uk

National Railway Museum tel: 01904 621261
www.nrm.org.uk

Tanfield Railway fax: 0191 3874784
www.tanfield-railway.co.uk

Timothy Hackworth Victorian and Railway Museum
tel: 01388 777999
www.hackworthmuseum.co.uk

Stephenson Railway Museum tel: 0191 2007145
www.twmuseums.org.uk/stephenson

Vintage Railway carriage Museum tel: 01535 680425
www.bradford.gov.uk

Wylam Railway Museum tel: 01661 852174
www.northumberland.gov.uk/vg/railway.html

George Stephenson's Cottage tel: 01661 853457
www.northumberland.gov.uk/vg/railway.html

SHIPS AND ENGINEERING

Discovery Museum tel: 0191 2326789
www.twmuseums.org.uk/discovery

POWER STATIONS

Sellafield Visitors' Centre tel: 01946 727027
www.bnfl.com

Heysham Power Station Visitors' Centre tel: 01524 833624

SCOTLAND

STATIONARY STEAM ENGINES

Garlogie Mill Power House Museum tel: 01771 622906
www.airnautic.com/westhill/garlogie_mill.htm

The Museum of Lead Mining – Wanlockhead Beam Engine
tel: 01659 74387
www.leadminingmuseum.co.uk/beamenginepage.htm

Prestongrange Museum tel: 0131 6532904
www.eastlothian.gov.uk/museums

New Lanark World Heritage Centre tel: 01555 661345
www.newlanark.org

Verdant Works tel: 01382 221612
www.verdant-works.co.uk

Dunaskin Open Air Museum tel: 01292 531144
www.dunaskin.org.uk

Sumerlee Heritage Park tel: 01236 431261
www.northlan.gov.uk

Scottish Mining Museum tel: 0131 663 7519
www.scottishminingmuseum.com

RAILWAYS

Bo'ness and Kinniel Railway tel: 01506 822298
www.srps.org.uk

Caledonian Railway tel: 01561 377760
www.caledonianrailway.co.uk

Strathspey Steam Railway tel: 01479 810725
www.strathspeyrailway.co.uk

Royal Museum of Scotland tel: 0131 2474219
www.nms.ac.uk/royal/index.htm

Kinniel Estate and James Watt's Cottage tel: 01506 778530
www.falkirkmuseums.demon.co.uk/museums/kinnmus/htm

Museum of Transport tel: 0161 2052122
www.gmts.co.uk

SHIPS AND ENGINEERING

Scottish Maritime Museum – Irvine tel: 01294 278283
www.scottishmaritimemuseum.org

Aberdeen Maritime Museum tel: 01224 337700
www.aagm.co.uk

Scottish Maritime Museum – Clydebuilt tel: 0141 8851441
www.scottishmaritimemuseum.org

Royal Yacht Britannia
www.royalyachtbritannia.co.uk

INDEX

Page numbers in *italics* refer to illustrations

PICTURE CREDITS

BBC Worldwide would like to thank the following for providing photographs and for permission to reproduce copyright material. While every effort has been made to trace and acknowledge copyright holders, we would like to apologize should there be any errors or omissions.
C: centre, l: left, r: right, tl: top left, tr: top right, bl: bottom left, br: bottom right

Colour section one: Birmingham Central Library Archives: p.2(t); David Hall: p.7(b); Historical Picture Archive/Corbis: p.5(b); Mary Evans Picture Library: p.1(b), p.2(b), p.4(t), p.5(t), p.8(both); National Railway Museum/Science and Society Picture Library: p.6(b); Science Photo Library: p.4(b), p.7(t); Science Photo Library/Dr Jeremy Burgess: p.6(t); Science Photo Library/Sheila Terry: p.1(c); Science Museum/Science and Society Picture Library: p.1(tl), p.3.
Colour section two: Mary Evans Picture Library: p.1(tr); David Hall: pp.2–3, pp.4–5, p6; Hulton Archive/Getty Images: p.1(b); Hulton Archive/Getty Images/William Vanderson: p.7; Science Photo Library: p.1(tl); National Railway Museum: Science and Society Picture Library: p.8(both).
Colour section three: Mary Evans Picture Library: p.2(t), p.3, p.4(t), p.5(both); David Hall: p.2(b); Science Museum/Science and Society Picture Library: p.1, p.4(b), p.6(both); Stuart Wood/BBC Worldwide: p.7(both), p.8.
Colour section four: Corbis: p.3(br), p.8(t); Hulton-Deutsch Collection/Corbis: p.5; David Lees/Corbis: p.3(bl); Mary Evans Picture Library: p.2(b); Mary Evans Picture Library/Royal Institution of Civil Engineers: p.2(t); David Hall: pp.6–7; National Maritime Museum: p.1(t); National Museum of Photography, Film and Television/Science and Society Picture Library: p.4; Science Museum/Science and Society Picture Library: p.1(b), p.3(t); Stuart Wood/BBC Worldwide: p.8(b).
Illustrations within text pages: Bettmann/Corbis: p.91; Mary Evans Picture Library: p.21, p.78, p.105, p.107, p.113, p.119, p.134, p.135, p.151, p.175; Science Photo Library: p.37, p.85; Science Photo Library/Dr Jeremy Burgess: p.52, Science Photo Library/Sheila Terry: p.62; Science and Society Picture Library: p.26, p.136, p.141, p.144; Steam Engine Library, Department of History, University of Rochester: p.14, p.16, p.47.